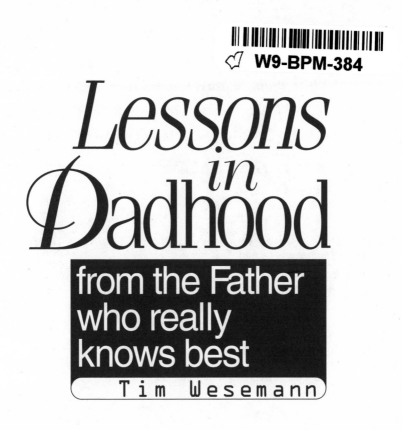

Lessons in Dadhood

from the Father who really knows best

Tim Wesemann

CPH.

SAINT LOUIS

To Benjamin, Sarah, and Christopher,
gifts from heaven who call me Dad.
In Christ's love you will find my love for you.

Material from *Through the Wilderness of Loneliness* © 1991 by Tim Hansel.
Used by permission of Chariot Family Publishing.

The melody of "You Are by My Side" © 1991 Concordia Publishing House.

Material from "A Tribute to Dads," which first appeared in *Just Between Us*
(Spring 1995), used by permission of the author, Jan Frans.

Material from "Dear Mom" first appeared in *Lutheran Witness* (May 1993).
Used by permission.

Scripture quotations are taken from the HOLY BIBLE, NEW INTERNATIONAL VERSION®.
NIV®. Copyright © 1973, 1978, 1984 by International Bible Society.
Used by permission of Zondervan Publishing House. All rights reserved.

Copyright © 1997 Concordia Publishing House
3558 S. Jefferson Avenue, St. Louis, MO 63118-3968
Manufactured in the United States of America

Library of Congress Cataloging-in-Publication Data

Wesemann, Tim, 1960–
    Lessons in dadhood from the Father who really knows best / Tim Wesemann.
      p. cm.
    ISBN 0-570-04885-0
    1. Fatherhood. 2. Fatherhood—Religious aspects—Christianity. 3. Fathers—
United States. I. Title.
HQ756.W45 1997   96-45187
306.874'2—dc21

1 2 3 4 5 6 7 8 9 10   06 05 04 03 02 01 00 99 98 97

Contents

As You Begin

What a joy to write these devotions! They have helped me grow in my relationship with my heavenly Father. This project has also caused me to realize—all over again—what a precious gift my children are. In my 10 years of fatherhood, I've realized that I am blessed, but I also have much to learn. I am thankful for the lessons God provided through this work.

There was an ironic twist to putting this book together. One day while I was working at my computer, my children kept coming in to ask if I could play. Trying to focus on my writing, I got a little frustrated and firmly said, "No, I can't play now! I have to write these devotions for dads." I started laughing and asked myself, What's wrong with this picture? Then I apologized and went out to play. Fatherhood—what a wonderful journey! I pray our Father in heaven brings us all great joy as we journey with Him in this high calling as Christian parents.

As you read each devotion, you'll find a Scripture reference for more digging. I've concluded each devotion with a short prayer or prayer idea under the heading "Father to Father." Dads, I hope you'll also enjoy the "God's Man in Action" suggestions. They are intended to help you carry God's message with you and put it to work in your daily life.

I would like to thank the following people who have been instrumental in this project:

- Ruth Geisler and Concordia Publishing House for opening this window of opportunity and letting the Son in.

- Lynn Hemphill for her keen eye for typos, at least until her eye suddenly focused on her new grandchild.

- Randy and Linda Rogers who acted as a test couple for the manuscript.

- The members I serve at Salem Lutheran Church and School, Affton, Missouri, and those I formerly served at Zion Lutheran Church, Pevely, Missouri. As extended family, you have been a supportive blessing to my family. You are truly appreciated!

- My father, whom I am eager to meet in heaven. We have an eternity to get to know each other while we praise our heavenly Father and His Son, Jesus Christ.

- My mom, who took on the role of Christian mother *and* father. She taught me daily and eternal lessons for which I am grateful. While your lives go on in heaven, Mom and Dad, your lives continue here on earth through our family.

- My wife, Chiara, who stayed up late reading these pages and giving support and encouragement. Thank you for everything you teach me about parenting. What a blessing to walk with you, sharing a common love for the children God has entrusted to our care.

- Our children—Benjamin, Sarah, and Christopher—without whom I would not be able to write a book about dads. I love you! You light up our home and lives. We are honored to be your parents and are overjoyed to witness the Lord bringing out His best in you.

- My brothers and sister and the other moms and dads God has placed in my life. You are a part of who I am.
- My Father, who art in heaven … hallowed be Thy name forever and ever. And eternal praise to His Son, the world's Savior, Jesus Christ. To God alone be the glory!

Tim Wesemann
Father's Day Weekend 1996

Wrapped around Her Little Finger

Isaiah 53:4–5

First a *thud!* Then a cry ... more like a wail! I went running. It was serious because the crying and the tears were coming from a little girl—my little girl. It's always serious when that's the scenario. The damage? Just a scraped knee—nothing too serious.

My wife and I tried all the boo-boo distraction tactics we knew. We called for boo-boo bunny. We cried with her. We held her tight and sang feel-good songs in her ear. Our efforts seemed to make it worse. What was left? A bandage?

"Yyyeeesss!" came the reply.

Could it really by that simple? I ran and grabbed one with her favorite cartoon character on it. We started to place it over her scraped knee, but Sarah let out another scream, "Noooooooooo!"

"But I thought you wanted a bandage?"

"I (sniffle, sniffle) do." With that she held out the little finger on her right hand.

"But, sweetheart, you hurt your knee, not your finger."

"WWWhhhhhhaaaaaaaaaaa!"

She won. The bandage was swiftly wrapped around her little finger. Immediately the crying stopped, except for those little postcrying gasps that have no name. She wiped her eyes with her sleeve. Everything was fine.

To this day I'm not sure I'll ever understand that one. I'm thinking of having this case written up in the *Harvard Journal of Boo-Boos*!

Sarah was miraculously satisfied when the bandage was wrapped around her finger even though her knee was left uncovered and a trickle of blood ran down her leg. With that substitutionary act, life was full, happy, and back to normal.

I scratched my head as Sarah walked away, and God scratched at the door of my heart. Through His Word, He reminded me of all my boo-boos—*sin* is the word He uses. He reminded me of my tears. He reminded me of the times I have tried to justify my sins, hide them, and forget them. But that didn't work. Although my sins were against God, through them I also had hurt others. The sins occurred in every aspect of my life, yet Jesus took me somewhere else. He led me to a hill outside Jerusalem where we stood in the shadow of a cross. There He bandaged all my sins and wrapped His healing words around my heart and hurts.

He said, "Surely, I took up your infirmities and carried your sorrows. I was pierced for your transgressions. I was crushed for your iniquities. The punishment that brought you peace was upon Me, and by My wounds you are healed" (based on Isaiah 53:4–5).

He won! The bandage of forgiveness was swiftly wrapped around my life, and immediately my sins and their scars were removed and forgotten. He wiped my tears on His blood-stained sleeve. All that remained were those little postforgiveness gasps of thankfulness.

I'm not sure I'll ever understand such grace. But it's been written about in the Book of Life, and through God's Spirit, I believe. With Jesus' substitutionary act, my life is now full and happy. I walk forgiven because blood flowed from His life-giving body that hung on the cross.

Sarah may have a bandage (and me) wrapped around her little finger, but it's more important that Jesus has wrapped His cross around our lives as He forgives us, holds us, wipes our tears, and makes everything fine.

Father to Father: I may never fully understand Your grace, but thanks to the work of Your Holy Spirit within me, I accept it, rejoice in it, and respond to it by giving You my life. In Jesus' name. Amen.

God's Man in Action: Carry a bandage with you today. Use it as a reminder to thank your heavenly Father for healing the infirmity of your sin through His Son, Jesus Christ.

What's Come between Us?

Matthew 10:32–33

S chool was almost over. The pickeruppers were getting stationed in the appropriate spots. I was visiting with a friend and fellow father on the far end of the parking lot. When the bell was about to ring, I said good-bye and headed for the school. As I walked away, he said in a tone reminiscent of Winnie the Pooh's friend Eeyore, "You get to go all the way over to the school?"

"What do you mean?" I asked.

"My daughter won't let me pick her up right outside school. She asked me not to park too close to the school so she can come out with her friends without her dad there. She's a teenager, you know. Things sure have changed," he said. He got an Eeyorian look on his face to match the tone of his voice.

The school bell rang. My friend slipped into his car. Guilt accompanied me as I made my way toward the school to pick up my children. It was difficult to leave him at the far end of the parking lot. I wanted to look back to see if he was disguising himself with glasses and a fake mustache.

He wasn't the first father who said his children had

gone from seeing him as the greatest dad in the world to the most embarrassing dad in the world. I guess most of us go through stages like that. Some even experience greater extremes of separation. What once made little children giggle causes them to grimace when they reach a certain age. A little one's gleeful "Oh, Daddy!" soon changes to a drawn out, "Daaaad!" At certain ages a daughter loves to dance in her daddy's arms, but not when he comes to chaperon a school dance. As the years go by, even hugs can turn into don't-let-anyone-see-us events.

I realize not everyone goes through such stages. I pray that my children bypass them altogether. It must be an odd, hurtful feeling for dads.

Then again, I wonder how often I do that to my Father God? I hurt Him when I walk past without the simplest acknowledgment of His presence. How many times do I keep Him at a distance even though He's always close? When certain people are around, do I try to hide His presence in my life? Do I stiff arm His invitation to join Him in the joyful dance of life? Have my prayers to Him turned professional and formal rather than childlike with an "Abba!" greeting? Have I been leaving Him at the far side of the church parking lot on Sunday? Or, do I remember He is with me throughout each day and each situation?

Now it's my turn to hang my head in Eeyorian style. Yes, Father, I have hurt You with my sins of distance. At times my actions have given the impression that You don't matter or that You embarrass me. I want to boldly acknowledge Your presence in my life. More than that, may my ways and words profess You as Lord of my life.

I remember my fellow father's words, "Things sure have changed." Change is what I need in my relationship with my heavenly Father. May His Spirit draw me in for a better, closer relationship.

Father to Father: Father, I acknowledge my sin of distancing myself from You. I ask for Your forgiveness. Acknowledge the sacrifice of Your Son to cover my sins and bring me closer to You in every aspect of my life. In the name and sacrifice of Jesus I come to You. Amen.

God's Man in Action: Share a hug with your child today—in public and in private. Notice any difference? Plan to make a verbal acknowledgment of Your Father today in the presence of a co-worker, friend, or stranger.

Picture Perfect

When I sit at my office desk, my children surround me. Actually, their pictures surround me. To my right is Sarah, smiling from her homemade frame. Christopher and Alexander, the cat, sit just to her left. The funny, old-fashioned dress-up picture is on the top shelf. Right in front of me are the professional portraits. Under the glass on my desk is a family shot. To my left is a photo cutout of a good-night giggle. Just past that is Benjamin in younger days. Behind me is Christopher, struggling to open a cupcake wrapper. There's also one family picture in my wallet. I don't get to see that one very often, unless someone doesn't mind if I show it off.

I love being surrounded by my children. I'm proud of them. Their smiles make me smile. When we can't be together, this is a nice substitute. And because my wife has a talent for taking pictures, I have no shortage of wonderful prints to display. Unfortunately, it's not practical to take all these photographs with me.

Recently, I ran across a father who works as a fix-it man. His office is his toolbox. It goes everywhere he does. When I walked past his open toolbox, I noticed that several family pictures, complete with special notes, lined the inside top of the box. That day, his children not only made him smile, but this father too. That father carried his children with him wherever he went. I wanted to buy a toolbox for my pictures. (I could be the first pastor to make hospital visits with a toolbox!)

I love being surrounded by pictures of my children when the real thing isn't possible. I also love being surrounded by my Savior and His picture-perfect grace.

What reminisces the picture of Jesus pulling Peter out of the water bring. How can a person not be affected by the snapshot of the shepherds worshiping the Christ Child? Then there's that funny one of the Pharisees scratching their heads as Jesus walks away after telling a parable. Look at how this shot catches the intensity in Jesus' face as He eyes Satan and turns him away. The photo of Jesus' transfiguration is powerfully framed in His majesty. One of the most moving pictures is difficult to look at because the agony and pain are so vivid. It is Jesus on the cross. What really stands out is the color of grace in His eyes. Another favorite catches Him standing nearby as Mary cries because she thinks someone has stolen His body.

A set of favorites fills a five-picture frame. Each portrait is a picture of God the Father at a Baptism— my baptism, my wife's baptism, and the rebirth of each of our children. The camera caught Him just as He said, "These are My children, whom I love with all My heart. With them, because My Son's life covers them, I am well pleased."

What joy and strength come from being surrounded by the picture-perfect grace of our God. His vivid presence is with us in His Word, in our Baptism, and in His Holy Meal. What fun it is to take every opportunity to share His pictures with those who don't mind our bragging. "Let Him who boasts boast in the Lord!" I can picture that perfectly, can't you?

Father to Father: When people take pictures, they usually say, "Smile!" Father, when I take Your picture-perfect photographs of life with me, no one needs to say "Smile!" It comes naturally! Surround me and my family with Your strengthening love. In my Savior's name. Amen.

God's Man in Action: Get out the camera and take some family pictures today. They'll look good on your desk, in your toolbox, on your dashboard—wherever!

The Best There Ever Was

1 Corinthians 4:15

Children love bragging about how their father is the biggest, best, or most talented. That was one childhood game in which I didn't participate.

As I grew older, I found out many things about my father—he was a gifted, talented man. As I grew to know him, he became a favorite companion. We developed a unique parent-child bond of friendship, trust, and caring—whether laughing and sharing jokes, getting down to business man-to-man, or even disagreeing.

In my efforts to know this man, had I stumbled across the perfect father? By no means. But I tended to close the shade on any imperfections he had, letting faultless characteristics shine through.

My youthful days had passed by the time I finally began to know my father and to appreciate him. I even learned to love and respect my seemingly ageless dad. It was then, like a child, that I could brag that my father was the biggest, best, and most talented. In fact, he was the best there ever was.

My dad cared about what I cared about. He was attentive to my needs and concerns. He loved me and encouraged me. All this yet we never attended a father-son banquet. All this yet he never took the time to sign one of my report cards. All this and more, even though my father died four months before I was born.

Many children have the opportunity to grow up with the love of one father. But through my father's death, I found that God blessed me with many "fathers."

I didn't miss that parental figure during my childhood. I guess one doesn't miss what one doesn't know. Only after I began to search and question did the answers come. I have a father. In fact, I have many. He is the multi-faceted special friend and loving father in the people around me. When I need a father, he is there. He is any man who takes the time to love me as a son, friend, or child of God.

I never had the opportunity to know my father, but I thank God that He has blessed me with many "fathers" to fill that role. Most important, I thank Him for the relationship He created between us as perfect Father and less-than-perfect son.

Father to Father: Heavenly Father, how grateful this son is for Your perfect love and example. Make me a godly, fatherly example to others. In Jesus' name. Amen.

God's Man in Action: Pick up the phone, or pen and paper, and let the person who was an "additional father" to you know how much you appreciate his presence in your life.

Fix It!

Luke 18:27

We found two specials at the mall one evening. One was on shoes. The other was in the form of a clown who shaped balloons into poodles, flowers, swords, and more. Our children seemed quite impressed, even though I had made my own balloon creations for them at home recently. Okay, I admit that my snake and hot-dog shaped balloons left something to be desired, but I tried.

Balloon sculptures are an art form that one must appreciate quickly because they rarely last long. Such was the case with Benjamin's balloon. As soon as we got in the car, we heard a *pop,* followed by a moment of silence. Then came the "oh-h-h-h" sound, signaling deflating joy.

Before we could extend our sympathies, Benjamin spoke up. "Can you fix it?" Obviously, he had taken last night's game of "SuperParents" a bit too seriously.

Our class on consoling children failed us as my wife and I simply said, "No."

Benjamin had an idea. "But when we get home you could sew it back together!"

Some things are impossible to fix.

I really should rephrase that. Some things are impossible for humans to fix on their own. For many fathers, those are tough words to read. Some men have been struck with Tim-the-Tool-Man-itus. One of its symptoms is making statements like, "I can fix anything!"

Most fathers can't fix a daughter's heart that has been broken by her first love. It is next to impossible for fathers, on their own, to repair the damage caused by hurtful words hurled in anger at their children. No man can actually remove from his wife's memory degrading words that were spoken in frustration. Fathers cannot reverse time and change a decision to work late instead of attending a child's school program. No father can change the past. No father can save the soul of a family member—no *earthly* father, that is. No parent can fix a balloon sword with needle and thread. It's impossible.

But with God, our heavenly Father, nothing is impossible. Ask the aging Abraham and his hysterical wife, Sarah, about that. At their age the thought of pregnancy was inconceivable to them. Or, ask Mary or Joseph about the possibility of the impossible coming to life. Ask Saul's friends if they thought he could possibly become a star apostle for the Morning Star. Or, inquire of the rich ruler about the possibility of getting into heaven on his own. Dads cannot fix everything, be a savior. Jesus has taken care of that.

Daily, God's Holy Spirit invites us to enter a fix-it

shop where a Carpenter creates heavenly works. There the constant sound of nails being driven into a wooden cross echoes off the walls and enters the heart of our problems. The Carpenter's motto, which hangs on a beam, reads, "With Me nothing is impossible."

Notice that the room is filled with other fathers (and mothers and children) whose dreams have blown up in their faces. Pieces of lives are everywhere, and reconstruction seems impossible. Hurts and disappointments hang from bodies. But everyone has come to the right place. At this fix-it shop, forgiveness, hope, and salvation are the Carpenter's specialty. No wonder the cries of "Fix me, Savior!" go out as the life-giving cross goes up.

Father to Father: Fix me, Father! With You the possibilities are endless. In Your dear Son's name. Amen.

God's Man in Action: Surprise your family with a balloon or a bunch of balloons. If you stop in at a florist's, you also might find some flowers with your wife's name on them. And at home you can find time for that fix-it job with your name on it!

Psalm 23 Revisited

Psalm 23

Psalm 23 is one of the most recognizable and comforting passages of Scripture. Yet few fully understand the deepest meaning of the words. A lack of shepherd knowledge is partly to blame. With that in mind (and with all due respect to David, the Spirit-inspired author), I reworked the passage. I considered what would happen if my children exchanged the shepherding motif for the comfort of knowing the Lord as their daddy.

> The Lord is my Daddy, and that's really all I want. I love when I fall asleep in His arms and wake up in my bed. (I know He's the one who carried me there and tucked me in just right.)
>
> He makes sure I have everything I need— from pancakes to soda to Sunday school.
>
> Being with Him reminds me that I am someone special. With Him, I feel safe and secure.
>
> I love the feel of His daddy-sized hand surrounding mine when we're praying at church or when I'm surrounded by people— drowning in a sea of kneecaps.

Even in the middle of the deepest, most scari-
est darkness (the kind where you can't see
anything), His voice and His touch, they make
me feel all better.

Together, side-by-side, we walk past the
school bullies. They won't mess with my Dad!

We have such fun together. Sometimes my
cheeks hurt from smiling and laughing.

I love being part of this forever family!

Why should I limit this exercise to my children? This
is what I came up with as I stood in David's sandals
and considered my flock of children grazing on brown-
ies for dessert.

The Lord is my Father—talk about content-
ment! He teaches me how to relax and how
to pass that peace on to my family.

He took me to His living waters of Baptism.
Satan doesn't play in that water!

There He gave me gifts and assured me that
I am one of His gifts to my children. He
brings out His best in me and leads me, as I
lead my family, in His ways.

I know that nothing—not even death (or life
at its worst)—can come between me, or my
family, and His love. I have His Word on it.
So why should I worry or be afraid? I won't!
He is with me. He gives me strength and

hope. He even gives me wisdom to handle those deep questions that only a preschooler can concoct.

Satan wants to bring me and my family down, but the Lord has set up shop in the middle of our home and lives.

When I am hurting, anxious, or feeling guilty, He applies His Gospel salve and His healing touch of forgiveness.

I am overwhelmed by the joy that His presence and promises bring. I am one very blessed father because the Lord is my Father. Don't even think that this is a temporary situation. There's no doubt it's permanent.

Father to Father: Lord, You are my shepherd, that's all I want or need. Teach me to shepherd and to father as You do. As I dwell in Your house, come and dwell in mine. In Jesus' name. Amen.

God's Man in Action: Read Psalm 23 and John 10:1–18 and apply these passages to your life and family.

Father Job

Job 1:1–5

When you think about Job, your first thought probably is not *father*. It is more likely an image of a suffering man, sitting alone in a heap of ashes, scraping his sores with broken pottery.

The opening verses of the book of Job give tremendous insight into the family man and father. Job was blessed with 10 children—three daughters and seven sons. He showered his family with pets—seven thousand sheep, three thousand camels, and hundreds of oxen and donkeys.

The inspired story of Job begins with many, if not all, of his children grown and living in their own homes. They take turns having family dinner parties. This, in itself, suggests that Job and his wife had raised a family that respected and honored one another. What a blessing!

Job took his responsibilities as a God-pleasing father seriously. He loved his children and cared deeply about their faith. As was the custom after a feast, Job made sure his children were purified. He got up early and sacrificed a burnt offering for each child. If there was a possibility that his children had sinned against God, Job turned to God for their deliverance. Scripture tells us this was his regular custom.

We are often inspired by Job's faith as he endured the loss of his family, servants, crops, and animals. Job's world fell apart when he got word that all his children were crushed when the oldest son's house collapsed. His children died together, as a family. But Job's faith didn't collapse. Instead, he said, "Naked I came from my mother's womb, and naked I will depart. The Lord gave and the Lord has taken away; may the name of the Lord be praised" (Job 1:21). God tells us that, in all this, Job did not sin by charging God with wrongdoing. We stand in awe of his faith. We also can stand in awe of his fathering techniques.

Job put God first. In doing so, he recognized his serious and joyful calling as a God-pleasing father. He entrusted his family to God in their celebrating and in their working, in their living and in their dying.

Father to Father: May Your name be praised in my life, in my parenting, and in my walk with You. I praise You for Job—his exemplary life as Your child and as a faithful father. Help me proudly proclaim as he did, "I know that my Redeemer lives." In Jesus' name. Amen.

God's Man in Action: Plan a fun family night. Order out for supper, play games, and pray together as a family.

Wing It!

Exodus 19:4

As the due date for our first child grew closer, I could feel my anxiety level rise. (I know the women who are reading this over their husbands' shoulders are thinking what were you nervous about? Your wife did all the work! The point is well-taken.) I was more excited than nervous about the birth of our first child. But what worried me most was my delivery into fatherhood. That may sound self-centered, but let me explain.

I grew up without a father. My dad had gone to his Father in heaven while I was comfortably living in my mother's womb. Since my mother never remarried, I didn't have a father to take cues from. I didn't have the opportunity to record day-to-day fathering tips in my journal. My dad didn't have the opportunity to read me the book *How to Be a Father,* a book I was sure most other new dads had memorized. That was the reason for my concern.

My wife remembers hearing me say, "I don't know how to be a father. What does a father do? How am I supposed to act?" She told me to be myself and encouraged me about the gifts God had given me. Basically, she said, "Just wing it, Tim."

What? Soon a helpless human life would depend on us for everything, and she was telling me to wing it? The example I would set would affect this child for the rest of his or her life. I'm playing one of the most important roles in my child's life—and I should wing it?

Today I'm happy to announce that I'm the "experienced" father of three. If you're nervous about your ability to be a father—more than that, a Christian father—I offer this advice. (Do you have a highlighter to note this pearl of wisdom?) The advice is wing it! In fact, that is the advice I would give to anyone beginning a new venture, starting over, or just waking up to a new day that the Lord has created. My advice isn't original. It's scriptural.

In Exodus 19:4, the Lord told Moses to tell His Israelite children: "You yourselves have seen what I did to Egypt, and how I carried you on eagles' wings and brought you to Myself." The Lord was reminding His people of past victories. He wanted them to recall past adventures in which He had carried them on His wings, like an eagle, drawing them to Himself. His past record of support and power encouraged them as they walked into each situation. It is really God's advice, "Wing it—on My wings."

There is no better fathering tip than one from the perfect Father. His heavenly advice will fly in any adventure. Take the leap. Fly or fall. Our Father is there to take you and your family on the ride of your lives. Count on His presence. Plan on Him catching you when you fail. Hide under the protection of His wings as hurts roll off His feathers and your family goes unharmed. Let Him feed you as you learn to feed your children. Make sure that your daily flight plan includes a stop at an eagle refuge outside the city walls of Jerusalem (a cross marks the spot). Allow Him to do for you what He did for His Israelite children—He brought them to Himself.

The advice is simple yet vitally important. As you leap into fatherhood and as you soar into each new adventure-filled day—*wing it!*

Father to Father: Teach me to fly with You in all I do. Let's wing it together! In Jesus' name. Amen.

God's Man in Action: Keep your eyes open for a feather. Place it in a spot at home or at work where you most need to be reminded to "wing it" on God's wings.

Home Schooling

Ephesians 6:4

Home schooling is becoming a popular alternative to public and even private education. I haven't talked with many parents who are home schooling, but I stand in awe of their efforts. I would imagine that it takes commitment and knowledge, along with a healthy dose of patience. Once I had the opportunity to converse with a home-schooling mother. As I approached, I noticed that she was talking to herself. I think she was in the middle of a parent-teacher consultation. I thought it best not to interrupt.

God's Word notes an important aspect of home schooling, Christian-style. The Spirit-inspired author of Ephesians 6:4 tells fathers to bring up their children in the "training and instruction of the Lord." All fathers are called to home school when it comes to the subject of the Lord. As part of the relationship with his children, a father is to lead his family, with the blessing of the Holy Spirit, into a growing relationship with the heavenly Father. With fatherhood comes an additional hat to wear—that of teacher.

Teachers need certain tools and attributes to be effective. Instructors need to know their subject. In my view, the best teachers are the ones who also are committed to being students. It sounds like spending time at the feet of rabbi Jesus is in order.

Most classrooms include textbooks. God's Word is a necessity, others can assist.

Students need to feel free to ask questions. If teachers don't know the answers, it's best to reply honestly and search for the answers together.

A student won't learn if the teacher fails to show up. Taking time to instruct may seem obvious, but it's easy for father-teachers to find excuses to play hooky from teaching.

A variety of teaching techniques is always a plus. Learning from the teacher of all teachers, Jesus, we find He taught using objects, through parables, in one-on-one settings, on field trips, before large groups, and in a variety of other ways. Be creative as you share with your children the Good News that Jesus loved them enough to die for them.

The best teachers have a deep love and respect for their students. If you don't respect your children as dearly loved, chosen, and redeemed creations of God, how can you teach them about God's great respect for them? It's difficult for students to grasp the meaning of a lesson on God's unconditional love when the instructor fails to live the lesson that's being taught.

Home schooling is a must for Christian parents. Here's a lesson plan for the week.

Monday: New math with Peter—
The 70 × 7 Forgiveness Factor.

Tuesday: Home economics with Mary and
Martha.

Wednesday: Lunch special—
five loaves of bread, two fish, and one miracle.

Thursday: Recess at the Jordan River.

Friday: Class musical: Singing with the Angels.

Saturday: Field trip to Emmaus.

Sunday: Pep rally for team members running
the race.

Father to Father: Rabbi, I have been called to instruct my children in Your ways. Teach me Your ways so I can better instruct my children about our Father. Amen.

God's Man in Action: Give your children an apple from their teacher. Then take time to share, study, or pray as you instruct them in the ways of the Lord. Think about teachers and their techniques that were the greatest blessing to you. Apply those techniques as you instruct.

Untitled

Isaiah 45:4

If today were a chapter in my life, I'd have to title it "Untitled." It was my day off. My wife and children were out of town. I didn't do anything.

As I laid my head on the pillow, I realized I had been a good-for-nothing bum. The day seemed wasted. I hadn't crossed one thing off my "Honey do" list. I ate leftovers so there wouldn't be any "real" cooking to do besides pushing a few microwave buttons. I took a nap. (Pushing those buttons can really wear a guy out!) The TV worked overtime on my untitled day. I even used all the hot water in a skin-pruning shower. Then it was time for bed. Where had the day gone?

Have you ever had one of those days? Come on, admit it—please! I can't stand the guilt if I'm the only one. (Thank you.)

You know, during my untitled day, I was more than lazy. I was unfaithful to God. I don't remember issuing one prayer (not even for a little zest). I didn't turn a page in my Bible. I don't remember sharing God's love with anyone. I made fun of an actor on a silly television commercial. When the dog started barking, I barked back. What an ugly, useless day!

Now, I'm not promoting laziness. Believe me, these untitled days are few and far between—thank goodness! But the Lord taught me something about His love for me as I lay me down to sleep that night.

As I went to bed on that untitled night, I noticed my Bible, lying open on the nightstand. I noticed it because there wasn't room for my Twinkie and fruit punch (a perfect way to cap off any day). I had to move the open book to make room for my midnight snack. As I moved it, my eyes glimpsed Isaiah 45:4: "For the sake of Jacob my servant, of Israel my chosen, I call you by name and bestow on you a title of honor, though you do not acknowledge Me."

Suddenly I lost my taste for a snack. I was on holy ground. God was speaking to me. For the sake of Jacob, God acknowledged King Cyrus, even though Cyrus didn't acknowledge God.

I looked down again. This time it seemed to read differently. *"Timothy, for the sake of Jesus, My Son, your Savior, I have called you by name and bestow on you a title of honor, even though you did not acknowledge Me today."*

I put the snack on the floor and returned the Bible to the nightstand. I turned off the TV and the light. I prayed: "Forgive me, Father, for the sake of Jesus, Your Son, my Savior, for my sins of laziness, unfaithfulness, and for attempting to leave You out of this day that You entrusted to my care. But thank You for Your grace … even though I failed to acknowledge You today."

What a day this had turned out to be! This was a day that the Lord had made! I was glad and rejoiced in it. God has called me by name and made me His. I am God's child. What a title of honor! I think I'll retitle this brief chapter of my life: "Titled." It has a nice, true ring to it.

I can't wait to see what God titles tomorrow.

Father to Father: Use the prayer within this devotion.

God's Man in Action: As you go to bed tonight, open your Bible and read the pages in front of you. See what God has to say to you, His man of honor, on this "titled" day.

A Visit to a Construction Site

Genesis 11:1–9

I remember being intrigued as a child by a factory being built near my house. I was amazed at how the crew worked together to create this building where every beam, nail, and wire ended up right where it needed to be. I enjoyed watching their progress.

The only other construction site I visited during my childhood was one my Sunday school took me to. As I remember, we took a Bible trip to a site called Babel. People had gathered there to build a city. Their plans included a tower that reached to the heavens. They built the tower and the city to make a name for themselves. But their amazing plan had some major problems. First, they forgot to use an architect in their plans—an architect who had designed and created a flawless world. Second, they tried to build the tower by themselves, for themselves. They wanted the glory, the power, the name recognition.

God decided to include Himself in their selfish plans. He came down and confused their language so they couldn't understand one another. A safe, sturdy building can't be built without communication.

We spend a lot of time at a construction site. God is

constructing our Christian home. He is the architect and uses us as His workers to build a Christian home for our family. He has the plans laid out clearly on paper—an inspired plan. (We have His Word on it.) The foundation is built on Jesus Christ. The materials are the best of love, honesty, trust, joy, respect, peace, and honor. Daily we are to work on the holy ground of this construction site called our Christian home.

As we build, Satan notices what's happening. He wants to halt construction. He borrows a plan similar to the one God used at Babel. He causes communication problems at the construction site. Satan tempts us with a sinful breakdown of communication between Mom and Dad, parents and children, brothers and sisters, between family and Architect.

When communication breaks down within Christian homes, the construction work breaks down too. Sometimes Satan confuses our language, causing us not to honor one another. Often he plugs our ears so that we fail to listen to one another, an important part of communication. Trying his best to cause failed communication with God, Satan tempts us to focus on ourselves, not on God.

Satan's tools are scattered around the construction site. His hammer pounds bitterness into our hearts. His vices tempt us. His saw can reduce even solid relationships to tiny pieces. Satan's fake level gives a false impression of balance in our lives. He whittles down our relationships with sharp tools of jealousy, out-of-control anger, spite, and vengeance. Hurtful words are his nails. Satan has a blast at the construction site of the Christian home.

But God is the true architect and master builder of the Christian home. His plans overpower Satan. He communicated this perfectly at another site where nails and wood are found. On that wood, where Roman nails pinned Jesus to the cross, we find a reconciliation that builds relationships—between God and humans, between men and women, between children and parents, within homes and hearts. What a site to behold and hold on to as God builds our Christian home!

Father to Father: Dear Architect, don't let Satan (or me) get in the way as Your Spirit builds our Christian home on the firm foundation of Jesus Christ. Amen.

God's Man in Action: As a family, construct a simple cross made from wood scraps or broken branches. Place it in a visible spot and pray for successful construction in your Christian home.

I Have Had Enough!

1 Kings 19:1–9

Under a tree is an appropriate place to find a man of God.

That's where we find Elijah at one point in his life—under a tree. Elijah was on the run for his life, hunted by Jezebel and her army. He was living in fear. The chase took him into a desert. He kept moving, trying to outrun his enemies. But there, in the middle of the desert, he found a tree. Completely exhausted, he sat under it and prayed that he might die. "I have had enough, Lord," he said. Then he lay down under the tree and feel asleep.

Does the story sound familiar? Have you heard about other men of God in Elijah's place? Or, is it familiar because you have lived it?

The Jezebels in our lives are numerous. Satan loves to put on his Jezebel costume and take a run at us. Sometimes he takes the form of the bill collector. At other times, we are worn down by the pressure of raising children in a world that mocks God's Word. Fear of losing our job, or being too long without one, can push us into the desert. Stress in our marriage can make it seem like our wife is leading the attack against us. Sometimes we find that we are viciously chasing ourselves into the desert.

Fear paralyzes us. Unresolved anger breaks our stride. Guilt wears us down. Pressures of all kinds trip us up. It's not long before we find ourselves trying to survive in a desert wasteland. We have lost all zest for moving forward. Our cry goes up in despair, "I have had enough, Lord!"

God didn't leave Elijah there to die. He sent an angel. He sent a heavenly cake and water for nourishment. God allowed Elijah to rest and be refreshed. And don't forget the importance of the shade tree God provided in the heat of the day. Strengthened, Elijah traveled on until he reached the mountain of God.

In the middle of a desert journey, under a tree (with a cross beam) is an appropriate place to find a man of God in need of God's nourishment. I'll see you there.

Father to Father: Father, in the heat of this day I hear my enemies approaching. Thank You for providing the tree of life in the middle of my desert journey. Give me the power to continue traveling until I reach Your holy mountain. In the name of Jesus I pray and journey. Amen.

God's Man in Action: Draw a small cross on the tip of your running shoes. When you wear them, remember the peace God provides under a tree in the shape of a cross.

You're Welcome! Thank You!

Luke 17:11–19

I have found out that it's not always easy to teach a child how to respond appropriately.

Witness this scene. Our daughter, Sarah, kicked her older brother. Benjamin didn't take long to respond. Like any normal child, he yelled at his sister and then ran to Mommy and Daddy to make sure she was dealt with. The first part of our response was (all together now), "Sarah, what do you say to Benjamin?"

Her response? "Umm ... you're welcome! No, wait, umm ... oh, yeah, thank you!"

"No, Sarah," I reminded her, "I'm sorry!"

"Oh, it's okay, Daddy," she said, scampering off to her room.

Obviously Sarah's response mechanism had a short in it and teaching her to respond appropriately would take a little longer than we had hoped. I have a feeling that my heavenly Father understood what I was going through that day. He's raised a few children Himself (in more ways than one!).

Witness another scene. There were 10 men who were dying. They were physically dying from an awful skin disease. They also were dying for someone to welcome them into a conversation, a home, or a community. They had been banished outside the city limits because of their disease. Finally, they met the man who would change their lives. From a distance they yelled to Him for mercy, pleading for a welcoming word. He gave them that word and more. He sent them to the high priest who would welcome them back to their families and community because they had been miraculously healed. But nine of the 10 had more than a short in their response mechanism—it seemed nonexistent.

One had it right, even though it may have sounded wrong. Jesus had said to them, "You're welcome!" And one of the men who had been given new life came running back to Jesus to respond, "Thank You!"

God has graciously carried us over the welcome mat into His kingdom. We sometimes seem confused about how we are to respond to His love.

We have to remember that this is God's kingdom— His kingdom of grace where things often are done differently than how we do them on earth. Remember that this is the kingdom where the last shall be first and the first shall be last. In this kingdom the master is called to be the servant of all. This is a kingdom where "you're welcome" comes before "thank you," and "thank you" is a response to "you're welcome."

Our gracious God welcomes us to each new day that He has created. He welcomes us into hours of living in and by His grace. He welcomes us through His Word,

His sacraments, and His people. He welcomes us to help ourselves to a bit of heaven on earth through His presence with us, until we are welcomed into His eternal heaven. Throughout our day, He shouts to us, "You're welcome!"

And what do we say to Jesus? All together now:

"Thank You! Thank You! Thank You!"

Father to Father: Thank You! Thank You for Your daily and eternal welcome!

God's Man in Action: Be aware of how often you are welcomed today by mats on the floor, voices behind desks, signs on doors, speakers at drive-up windows, by family, by co-workers, and by friends. As you are welcomed, take a second to remember God's daily and eternal "welcome" and whisper, "Thank You!"

Grace *Du Jour*

Psalm 107:1

I 've observed that I am a very unobservant person. So many details pass by me. I'm thankful my wife doesn't change hairstyles or I'd be in trouble.

But I'm praying that the Creator will help me enjoy and appreciate more of His creation. I'm sure I miss so much that I should give thanks for. I know I take many of God's gifts for granted—unless they break, are lost, or fail me. Then I take immediate notice!

Let's call these precious gifts "grace *du jour*"— additional, taken-for-granted, daily blessings from the hand of a most gracious God. So my prayer today is "How thankful I am for Your grace *du jour,* Lord. Forgive me for taking You and Your daily gifts for granted. Lord, I must express my deepest thanks and gratitude to You for

- my wife's love, my children's smiles, and the reflection of You I see in their faith;
- alarm clocks with snooze buttons;
- pants with elastic waists and time to waste;
- photographs that bring memories to mind and minds that can bring back memories without photographs;

- my car engine that could and my prayers when it won't;
- telephone lines and grocery checkouts without lines;
- floppy, compact, and spinal disks;
- big bear hugs and little tugs on your sleeve you can't bear to ignore;
- regular trash pickup and spiritual pick-me-ups;
- baby coos and honey-dos;
- pizza, paper, and miraculous deliveries;
- belly laughs and jokes that produce them;
- chocolate;
- paychecks and paid-off loans;
- invocations and benedictions (and everything in between);
- and for grace *du jour* and a Savior who takes that grace and feeds the multitudes."

Father to Father: Use this prayer or write your own.

God's Man in Action: List people or things you're thankful for that you may have taken for granted in the last hour. Add them to your prayer *du jour* list.

Initial Success

Matthew 26:36–46

From NYC, NY, to LA, CA, and throughout the U.S., initials and abbrs. have come to find a perm. place in our Eng. language. We are OD-ing on initials, abbreviations, and shortened words. Ea. sec. of our A.M. and P.M. hrs. is filled w/initial successes.

From the moment we are born (in the OR, OB ward, with a Dr. & R.N. by our mother's side) to the moment we're 6 ft. under and 6 in. in the obits (may we R.I.P.), we eat, sleep, drink, etc., init. & abbrs.

Religion isn't exempt. At Sun. services, the Rev. reads an OT or NT text from the Bible—NIV, RSV, KJV, or another trans. We have family devos, reading selections from Gen. to Rev. in the comfort of our 3 BR, 2 ½ BA, br. home (w A/C).

Initially, I thought this phenomenon in the fast-paced, look-for-shortcuts world was great. But the longer I thought about it, the more I realized shortening isn't *always* better.

What a blessing to have Christian publishing companies that realize the need for materials that allow us to be built up spiritually while living in an on-the-go world. On the other hand, we can begin to get very comfortable being fed spiritually with the speed of a fax message. Then it becomes easy for Satan to quickly lead us away from worship time with our Lord and families. In our microwave world we can easily attend worship with one eye on the clock and the other straining to focus on Christ. So many of us live on fast food that we figure our faith likes fast soul food.

"Initial" success also hits our calling as husbands, fathers, and Christian friends within the body of Christ. Often we find ourselves with little time, energy, or desire for anything because we're so preoccupied with everything.

It is vital, initially and eternally, to follow God's way. That means taking the time to grow in the love of our Savior. That love is seen in what has been described as "the Gospel in a nutshell" (yes, it's short and sweet), John 3:16: "For God so loved the world that He gave His one and only Son, that whoever believes in Him shall not perish but have eternal life." That is an eternal, loving message to grow in—not *when* we have the time but *as* we take the time.

God's love story began before the foundation of the world. It was at that time that God initially chose us (Ephesians 1:4). We were chosen, loved, designed, planned with a purpose, and graciously handpicked to be holy and blameless in God's sight—initially—before the creation of the world. God's love story climaxed on Calvary's cross, where we were made holy and blameless through Jesus Christ. His saving love came to life within us when His Spirit created faith in us. What a timely message of hope to a hopelessly frantic world.

Father to Father: Lord, I pray that when You speak to me today, Your words are not the same ones Your disciples heard: "Could you not keep watch with Me for one hour?" I look forward to spending time with You every day, my precious friend. Forgive my shortcomings. Thank You for granting me initial and eternal success entirely because of Your timeless love. Amen.

God's Man in Action: Clear a block of time and plan to spend additional time alone with Your timeless God in prayer, meditation, and worship. Get rid of distractions that would interrupt you.

Beaten and Robed

Luke 15:11–32

Yesterday was one of those days. I was beaten. It wasn't a physical beating but a beating from Satan and his games. He beat me at hide-and-seek (the keys); bumper cars (on the highway); hot potato (under the collar); go fish (and get hooked in the ear); and water tag (when the dishwasher leaks).

By day's end, not only had I lost my keys and almost an ear, but I had lost my temper, my patience, my self-control, and my wits. That's why I found so much solace in Jesus' parable about a man who had been beaten. More than that, he had been beaten and robed. Check it out—the story of the prodigal son (Luke 15:11–32).

The youngest son had been beaten. He had been beaten by Satan and his world of fun and games. He hit bottom and he realized it.

The Master Storyteller tells us that when the young man came to his senses, he decided to go back to his father, repent, and ask to be a hired hand because he didn't deserve to be accepted as a son. After all, he had squandered the inheritance he had requested from his father. The younger son bid farewell to the pigs and the life that had beaten him, and he headed home.

Grace is obvious in the image of the father running with his arms and heart open to his son. The father grants acceptance even before repentance. Then comes the welcome, the clothes, the ring, and the party. His son was dead but is alive again. He was lost but now is found.

Back up for a bit. We passed over a very important act of the father's love. Take a longer look at the father's desire for his son to wear the best robe. The best robe in the house would have belonged to the father. But the father wanted the best for his son, so he covered his son's beaten body and bruised image with his own robe. The son who was once beaten is now robed. He has been covered by his father's best.

The story is familiar, not only because we have heard it often but because it is the story of our Father's love for us. Do you realize what love the Father has lavished on you, that you should be called a child of God? (And that is what you are—see 1 John 3:1.) The obvious and vitally important grace is evident in His calling you. It is evident in His suffering and dying for you. It is evident in His resurrection for you. It is evident in the forgiveness He has won for you. It is evident on every page and chapter of your life.

The story of the prodigal son and your story, as well as mine, could be summed up in the simple fact that we were once beaten, but now we're robed. That's the story of our eternal life.

Jesus' blood was shed for sinners feeling the effects of being beaten by Satan's deadly games. The robes that have been custom-fit and ordered before the creation of the world are ready. There is a flurry of activity as the Father runs toward us, His compassionate heart beating faster. His arms are flung open, ready to embrace. "Quick!" He says, "Bring the best robe—My robe—and put it on My child whom I love."

Go ahead—put it on. It's His gift to you. Let the celebration and thanksgiving begin.

Father to Father: Father, I love Your gift. It is a perfect fit. Thank You. I love You too. In Jesus' name. Amen.

God's Man in Action: As your child prepares for bed, put your robe on him or her and read the story of the prodigal son. Then open your arms and your heart as together you talk to your heavenly Father.

Praise the Lord
in a Garden of Joy

Psalm 150

O ne summer, my wife, Chiara, decided to dedicate a portion of her garden to our children. They could pick what to plant, care for it, and reap the harvest of God's miracle of plant and vegetable life.

When Benjamin was asked what he would like to plant in his section, he quickly replied, "Mashed potatoes!" I hoped he would generously share with his dad if it worked.

The practical, no-fun adult in us would be tempted to quickly respond, "No, Benjamin, you can't do that. Pick something else." Hey! Lighten up before squelching a fun, creative idea. Mashed potatoes—why not? So what if the neighbors see you. In fact, you'll need an ice-cream stick marker that says *Mashed Potatoes*. Let's praise the Lord with a fun garden complete with mashed potatoes and maybe some chocolate-chip cookie plants while we're at it. Who knows how the Lord might surprise us when we get on our knees to see the miracles that have popped out of the ground.

As adults we need to be in sync with our child's faith and sense of joy. I love considering God's joy when He did some planting of His own. Who would have thought that something great could come out of that little town of Bethlehem? And Nathaniel learned that something good *could* come out of Nazareth. Have you ever considered how the people responded when Jesus decided to plant Saul in His garden?

Think about the reasons God decided to plant you where you are. Don't underestimate God or His ability to work miracles. Don't underestimate your ability to praise Him as He deserves to be praised. Praise God for causing your faith to grow in what you sometimes think is an unproductive garden.

I love to reflect on the Lord's sense of humor. He's planted me in the middle of this wonderful family and said, "Grow into a father! I'll water you with My baptismal grace and nurture You with a life-giving, sin-forgiving meal I call My own. You'll grow in the fertile soil of My Word. I'll provide a great cloud of witnesses to surround you and be an example for you. And I will let My Son shine brightly upon you as you grow, reaching up towards My heaven."

God even has placed a piece of wood, in the shape of a cross, over the spot He planted me. It reads: "Timothy, My Redeemed Child." And here I grow—blooming, by His grace alone, where He has planted me. Who would have guessed?

What's next? The Bible tells us that God's people did

some radical things in response to His creativity and power. They would praise the Lord in the sanctuary with trumpets and harps, with tambourines and dancing, with the clash of cymbals, with resounding cymbals. Some people are uncomfortable with too many church symbols in the sanctuary. Imagine what they would do if you started a church cymbal choir. They might grow into the kind of radical people God had in mind when He created them. They might just praise the Lord like never before.

Don't underestimate how God wants to use you. You may be His mashed-potato dad, planted in His garden of joy, who praises Him in all things.

Father to Father: Plant me wherever You would like, Father. Water me with Your living water and nourish me with Your eternal gifts. Cause me to grow, and with Your Spirit's help, I will give You praise in all things and in all my ways. I praise Your holy name. Amen.

God's Man in Action: If the season is right, pass on your second helping of mashed potatoes and plant them in a garden or clay pot. Don't forget to water it after you read Psalm 1.

The "I'ves" of March
(Or Any Month)

Romans 8:38–39

Dear Father in heaven,

I've had a difficult day.

I've been hurtful and hateful.

I've had a tough time dealing with those around me.

I've lost my patience with my family.

I've been uncommitted to follow in Your footsteps.

I've got habits that are hard to break.

I've been through the wringer and then put others through it by my lack of compassion.

I've been keeping so much inside, bottling it up.

I've been finding lots of excuses to run away.

I've been in a rut.

I've lost my zest for life.

I've realized I need help.

I've missed You.

Your child.

Dear child whom I love,

I've been waiting to hear from you because I have good news. I've got the answers for all your problems.

I've been watching you, crying for you, wanting to hold you. Yet when I come near, you push Me away.

I've missed you too.

I've always loved you and always will—don't shut Me out.

I've always loved your family. Follow My example as you lead and love them.

I've got the forgiveness that you need for your hateful and hurtful ways, for your lack of commitment and patience.

I've got what it takes to pull you out of your ruts and to put zest, zip, and zeal back into your days.

I've realized you need My help. I want you to know I never left. I want to help.

I've made an eternal commitment to you.

I've sent My only Son, Jesus Christ, to die in your place. That is how much I love you.

I've made sure that He took on Himself all your sins and the punishment you deserved so that you have hope and forgiveness as you live for Me.

I've given you a reason for living, and I have great plans for you.

I've missed you. Come, make yourself at home. You are always welcome here.

With love, your heavenly Father.

Father to Father: Pray "The I'ves of March" instead of just reading the words.

God's Man in Action: Write a letter to your heavenly Father that shares what's in your heart. Then read one of the letters He has written to you (suggestions: Philippians or Ephesians).

Bearing Fruit

John 15:1–17

When our son Benjamin was quite young, we planted an apple tree in the backyard. As soon at it was planted, he called his grandparents and explained, "Pop-Pop, we just planted an apple tree, and now we're going to put apples on it!"

I imagined the neighbors watching our family trying to attach apples to this sapling with duct tape, staplers, and glue guns. As humorous as this was, I realized it's not that uncommon a sight when it comes to bearing fruit in a spiritual, scriptural sense. It's very common for fruit-bearing Christians to take the credit for their fruitful good deeds. In John 15, Jesus makes it more than clear that we "bear fruit" only because we are connected to Him, the Vine.

I remember in high school art class, one required project was painting a still life. The teacher placed a bowl of fruit in front of us for inspiration. The picture of fruit that Jesus paints for us is not a still life. Rather, it is an active life connected to Him. The food of His Word proceeds from Him into the veins of each branch and leaf. Then fruit begins to grow into a luscious gift of food for someone else's nourishment. The vine must get due credit for bearing the fruit. The fruit does not have the ability to produce itself.

It is so easy to take the credit for the good fruit that we may have produced. And it is easy to blame the failures on someone else. Often, to look good, we will give superficial credit by attempting to attach the ripe fruit back on the tree. The truth must be exposed. There would be no fruit created without connection to the Vine.

Consider the children God has entrusted to you. What a blessing! We must first acknowledge that without the Vine, we would not have children. The blessing that they are and the good fruit they produce needs to be traced back farther than our roots as parents. We need to go back to the life-giving source. Then we give Jesus Christ the glory and the honor due His holy name.

We moved to another house after we planted that apple tree. I don't know if it's bearing fruit, but I'm thankful to watch God producing beautiful fruit through three young saplings planted in my house—named Benjamin, Sarah, and Christopher.

Father to Father: Father, by the power of Your Spirit, keep my family always close to You, firmly connected to the vine—Jesus Christ. Amen.

God's Man in Action: Take a fruit break today. As you do, consider its source and how it is nourished. Then give glory to its creator, the Vine.

Father Eli

1 Samuel 2:12

My heart has always gone out to Eli, the priest who was Samuel's mentor in the temple. But that isn't the only thing he was known for. Thanks to the inspired Word of God, everyone who reads the Old Testament finds out that Eli had two wicked sons. Other translations describe them as "corrupt," "evil," or "worthless." I think we get the picture. Wally and Theodore Cleaver they weren't.

Eli was the Lord's servant, but his sons were another story. The community knew the situation. Many conversations in town probably centered around Eli's evil sons. They had a reputation and it wasn't a positive one. That's tough on a parent.

Most likely, Eli spent many hours contemplating what he should have done differently while raising his sons. Embarrassment would have been a natural reaction at times. His feelings and emotions probably included anger that his sons were hurting his family and its name. He may have joked about his misbehaving sons with others to try and lighten the load. It wasn't funny though. The worst part was that they had no regard for the Lord. That fact hurt not only Eli but God and the people they served.

Eli isn't the only father to have children causing root rot on the family tree. Many can sympathize with Eli because they painfully walk in similar sandals.

The temptation for parents in similar situations is to not deal with it. Some give up because it takes too much effort or pain. Others convince themselves that all kids are disrespectful, hurtful, and basically corrupt. Some write it off as a "stage." Some dads grew up feeling worthless themselves and don't seem to know other options. Some feel they don't have the expertise or parenting skills to deal with the situation, so they do nothing.

When Eli was quite old, he finally spoke to his sons about their sinful behavior. Hophni and Phinehas didn't listen to their father's words of correction. Since they had little regard for the Lord, they probably had even less respect for their parents or anyone else.

We don't know the daily details of Eli's relationship with his sons, but we each know the daily details of our own relationships. Some of our fears, hurts, and concerns are known only to God. What a blessing to know that another Father, a heavenly one, knows our struggles. He is an expert in dealing with wayward children. When we look through His eyes, we even recognize ourselves as corrupt children of our heavenly Father. Suddenly the shoe is on the other foot.

So how does God the Father deal with His children who play with fire? He speaks openly and honestly to them about their sinful ways. In love, He addresses the issues head on and sends His Spirit to turn their hearts back home. He never gives up. He allows other family members to know of His children's ways so they can be encouragers, helpers, and ministers. He doesn't put off until tomorrow what He can do about the situation today. He will stop at nothing (even death on a cross) to win His children back. He leaves His perfect love as a pattern for their loving. He recognizes the frailty and importance of faith and wants to protect it and help it grow. Forgiveness and second chances are His forte. His love never ends.

Father to Father: Father, often my ways are evil and corrupt. I have shamed Your holy name and family. I come asking for forgiveness. Teach me to "father" as You do. Use me as an encourager to my children and to parents struggling with Eli-like problems. In Jesus' name. Amen.

God's Man in Action: Make a note that reads *Eli.* Let it be an acronym that reminds you to **E**ncourage, **L**ove all God's children, and **I**nvest quality time with your children.

Close Your Eyes and Take a Prayer

1 Thessalonians 5:17

Pastors are known for their Sunday afternoon naps. I am no exception. My family knows to include my nap time in most Sunday plans. Some pastors are known for leading their congregations in Sunday *morning* naps—I hope I am an exception to that.

As a youngster, I had a friend whose dad fell asleep almost every night after supper. One time his family took him to a movie. He fell asleep, snored, and talked in his sleep. They never took him a second time.

I loved when my children took naps. It was one way I could be a good example—I napped with them! Now that they're older, naps don't appeal to them. In fact, *my* naps don't always appeal to them. That's a real struggle for me.

There are times when I'm emotionally and physically exhausted. Those are the times when my children seem to have the greatest amount of energy, and they want me to share in it. Am I being a poor father if I choose to nap? When I decide to play with my kids instead of napping, my energy runs low and my patience dips. That's not fair to them either. What's a dad to do?

It's really a question of stewardship. On one hand, I can be a poor steward of the body and time God entrusted to me by staying up too late and being exhausted the next day. On the other hand, sleeping (and some naps are included in this) can show good stewardship of the body. Our bodies need rest, and our families need us.

I think there's another theological or spiritual issue connected to sleep, namely that sleep is a wonderful type of prayer. When the apostle Paul wrote to the saints at Thessalonica, he told them to pray continually. These words are important and powerful. What used to disturb me was the difficulty of praying continually when we, as humans, sleep. Then it hit me: A good night's sleep (or a good day's nap) can be one continual prayer to God.

Talk about beauty sleep. What a beautiful way to pray—with your eyes closed! When we take care of our bodies by getting enough sleep, we pray to God, "I care about this body You have entrusted to me. Thank You for this opportunity to rest it. I honor You with this sleep." As our bodies rest, our dreams and snores ascend to God as a prayer from His faithful stewards.

As humans, we need a certain amount of sleep to fully give God the glory He deserves when we're awake. What a blessing to know that our heavenly

Father hears all our prayers, whether awake or asleep. And God promises that He will not slumber or sleep. His ears are always attentive to the prayers of His faithful stewards who are praying continually.

The next time you are exhausted from work or play and need a nap or an early night, tell your family, "I'm going to the bedroom to take a prayer." Then go and pray continually with your eyes closed.

Father to Father: Creator Father, thank You for the gift of sleep. You have created me so my body needs to rest. Help me to be a faithful steward of this body and the time entrusted to me. Help me also to be faithful in my prayers—around the clock. In Jesus' name I bring these requests. Amen.

God's Man in Action: The next time you prepare to sleep, take time first for a verbal prayer and then ask God to bless the prayers you will offer as you sleep. Then, in the words of Martin Luther, "Go to sleep at once and in good cheer."

Last Words Are Lasting Words

1 Kings 2:1–3

L ast words are lasting words. If you have ever
been privy to someone's last words, I think you
will agree with that statement.

I will never forget the last words my mother spoke
to me before she died. In the last hours of her life, she
was heavily medicated and seemed comatose. Suddenly, she sat up in bed, looked at her children gathered
there, and said, "I love you, and I will see you again."
With those lasting words, she laid back down. A short
time later, when I was reading to her about heaven
from Revelation 21, her living soul was carried there.
Now I await the time when her final words are fulfilled
and I see her, my father, a large crowd of witnesses
who have gone before me, and my Savior, who makes
the eternal family reunion possible.

King David, knowing his death was near, shared
some last words with his son Solomon: "So be strong,
show yourself a man, and observe what the LORD your
God requires: Walk in His ways, and keep His decrees
and commands, His laws and requirements, as written
in the Law of Moses, so that you may prosper in all you
do and wherever you go." In other words, "Know God

and love Him. I love you and will see you again." These are wonderful words for parents to leave with their children, whether they are leaving for work or leaving this world.

David knew that his time to leave his son was near. He left Solomon with words to carry on. We don't always have that luxury, but we can live David's words every day with God's help. When we walk in God's strong ways, show ourselves to be men of God, and keep His decrees and commands, we will be communicating powerful, lasting words to our families—whether we live or die.

But even men of God fail in that commitment. As godly fathers and husbands, there are times we pray that the words we leave with our family are not our last words. That's why it's important that we have been privy to the last words of someone else. They were words of forgiveness for those who knew and those who failed to know what they were doing. These words told of salvation for all who turn to Him in repentance and trust. These words were spoken by a man who was truly thirsty because He was true man, sent to deliver living water to dehydrated souls. They come from a man who had to die forsaken so all who follow Him would not have to die alone or without hope. His last words shared with us the need to love those around us. His final words said that His Father's plan of salvation was finished—along with Satan's power—but a new, forgiven life would begin for those who believed the

Word. They were words of total commitment to His Father.

They are the last words of Jesus. They are lasting words. They are words that change our world. They make it possible for everyone who trusts in the one who spoke those words to last forever. They are lasting words for life.

Father to Father: Father, I love reading the words You have left for me. May they become my lasting words to pass on to my family and all I meet. In Jesus' lasting name. Amen.

God's Man in Action: Write a letter to your children and place it in a safe place with a message that it should be opened when you die. In it, point them to God, His lasting words of life, and to your heart that is filled with love for them.

Have Me Committed

Matthew 6:33

Fatherhood is an awesome calling. There is no doubt that much of what we do in our calling as fathers will affect our children throughout their lives. That is a powerful truth.

Consider how you were affected by the life of your father. Does the way that he communicated with your mother affect the way you now communicate? The same goes for how he dealt with frustration and anger. How often do you find that the words that come out of your mouth have an uncanny resemblance to your dad's words? How has your dad's faith or lack of it affected yours? Have you felt the affects of his love in the way you love? Compare your work ethic to that of your father. How influential has your dad's active presence in your life, or lack of presence, been as you father now? What traits do you share with your dad physically, emotionally, or spiritually?

Most often we are who we are because of what we learned in our homes. We are comfortable with what we know, and we continue in those ways. The Lord also has worked in our lives to take a negative childhood experience and use it in a positive way in our adulthood.

If we are honest, we are amazed at the powerful effect our fathers have had on us. Now we are fathers who are affecting the lives of our children. What an awesome responsibility!

We need to stand in awe of this calling and ministry. Dadhood calls for a great commitment from people who live in a world that seems to know little about that subject. Being a father takes energy and work, as do all relationships. We must face the reality that our ways will have a lifetime effect on our children.

Overwhelmed? Discouraged? Proud? Has the thought of inadequacy crossed your mind as you read these hard-hitting words? Know that help is not only on the way—it has arrived. Our heavenly Father points us to His Son. We are led into His presence for encouragement and help in the joyful task at hand. His promise is to walk with us through it all. Our Savior never said that He would leave us on the maternity floor or at the door to the adoption agency and then meet us later at the wedding reception. His promise is that when we commit our ways to Him, He will pour out His blessings. As we seek first His kingdom, He will place the riches of heaven at our feet.

God also calls us to find our adequacy in Him. When we look to ourselves or rely on our own strength in this monumental calling, we will find sin, failure, and inadequacy. We must keep our lives aligned with His and esteem Him for who He is. Then we find Him lifting us higher than we ever have been before.

Our heavenly Father promises forgiveness to His repentant people—earthly fathers included. With that gift, there is opportunity to right the wrongs we created in the lives of our children. He is the God of reconciliation. He is the healing God of scarred relationships. He is God. That says it all.

Setting Him apart—with help from His Spirit—as Lord in our hearts means He will bring out His best in us. When that occurs, we will have a God-pleasing, eternal effect on our children. What a joy to go into fatherhood eternally affected by our Father and His gifts of forgiveness, grace, and power.

Father to Father: Fatherhood is an awesome calling. You are an awesome God, awesome in Your fatherly love for us. I commit all that I am and have to You. In the name of Jesus I come. Amen.

God's Man in Action: When you are put on hold during a phone conversation, hold on to God's call to find your adequacy and esteem in Him.

Could You Survive Going Tubeless?

Exodus 20:3

Back in the early 1980s, several family-focused groups encouraged people to replace their television sets with family time. In many homes, the television has replaced the family altar. Television can easily become a god in homes. People have been known to schedule meal times, appointments, and family outings around TV shows. People sacrifice a lot to see a favorite program. Worshiping TV stars is not unusual.

I must admit that after college and during our first years of marriage, I watched too much television. Today, I could name very few prime time shows. I'm glad things have changed. Recently, I came across an embellished, humorous article I wrote for a regional newspaper. It was written tongue in cheek, but it is a reminder of how easy it is to put things before God. Here's a portion of the article.

I nearly dropped my rabbit ears when I heard about the trend that seems to be sweeping the nation—tube-ectomies! Are people really trying to survive without television? Some are going tubeless for a week, others a month, and still others are undergoing a complete tube-ectomy.

Can you imagine a whole month without TV? Why that's four hours of Abby Ewing scheming, at least 20 "Laverne and Shirley" reruns, 50 to 60 "Tonight Show" guests, 744 hours of CNN, and at least one telethon.

Stop! Don't go on! Uncle! I admit it. I am a product of the television generation.

My blender is hooked up to cable. I named my gerbils Nielson and Arbitron. I do the *TV Guide* crossword in pen. You think you can be in control without your remote control? You think it's easy putting your horizontal on hold for a month? What kind of fun sport would you be without your sports?

Don't knock a tube-ectomy till you try it, you say. I tried it recently when my little black-and-white passed on. After several boxes of tissues and even more hours of staring at a blank screen, I decided that if Walnut Grove could do without television, I could. It was useless. Suddenly my neighbors bore an uncanny resemblance to Fred and Ethel. The music on the radio sounded like Joanie and Chachi. I went to bed in the middle of prime time, and I dreamed of a brand-new, remote control, 24-inch color console.

By the time Donahue welcomed his guests the next morning, I already had welcomed a new set into my life.

Tube-ectomites argue that going tubeless will give families new life. The absence of TV will make families grow closer. Instead of watching "Hart to Hart," families can talk heart to heart. Without TV, families will have the time to do things together outside the TV room. They can play games, talk, cook out with the neighbors, and read ... just like the Waltons did.

But watch out. Sure, the Waltons seemed happy and secure without television, but look what happened to them—they were canceled.

Has the television stolen some of your precious family time this week? Cancel the notion that you will be canceled without it. Try channeling some of that extra time toward your family. It's difficult to hold a remote and a family conversation at the same time. Try setting down the remote while lifting up a Bible, a child, and a prayer. We need to put the control back into the loving, forgiving hands of our Savior who has a no-cancellation policy for His children.

Father to Father: Father God, it is my desire to love and trust in You above all things. I begin by relying on Your forgiveness, help, and grace. Your will be done. In Jesus' name. Amen.

God's Man in Action: Ready to sign up for a tube-ectomy? If television hasn't become a god for you, identify what has. Consider solutions to put God back where He belongs.

A Father's Tribute

1 Corinthians 1:18–24

L ooming over the city of Acapulco, Mexico, is a white cross. It juts out of the top of a mountain and can be seen from most spots of the city and its beautiful bays. It sits against a backdrop of blue Mexican sky. At night a cascade of lights illuminates it. During the day the bright sun reflects off the white paint, keeping it a focal point for residents and tourists. A church sits in the shadow of the cross.

This cross is more than an imposing structure on a hilly landscape. It was constructed by a father. He had it built as a memorial for his two sons who—if I translated the conversation correctly—died in a plane crash. The father has an ever-present and powerful reminder of the death of his sons. Unless he travels quite a distance, the cross will always be visible and the memory fresh. When the father and his family see the cross, I wonder if they remember the tragic way these young men died or the way that they lived? One thing is certain, the death of his sons will not be forgotten.

The father could have constructed a statue of his sons. He could have had a memorial built in the shape of the airplane in which they died. But he chose a cross like that on which the Savior of the world died. He chose a cross, which serves as a constant reminder of Jesus' death on our behalf. It is an empty cross symbolizing the resurrected, living Savior. The lights that surround the cross break through the darkest of hours. The cross rises against the backdrop of the heavens. It is seen by all, and at its base is a church where the Gospel of Jesus Christ is proclaimed.

What a great memorial indeed! It is the memory of the love of two fathers—the love of an earthly father and the love of the heavenly Father—who made living possible even amid death.

I would imagine that, especially for the people who live beneath that cross, it's easy to grow accustomed to it and barely even notice it. Unfortunately, it can be the same for us who live beneath Calvary's cross. It's tempting to take its grace-filled message for granted. It could be easy to walk by the cross week after week without being affected by its awesome message. Satan would love for us to see it as more of an eyesore and hindrance than the message of hope, forgiveness, and eternal life that it is.

Maybe that's why the boys' father built such an immense cross. Was he hoping that he would never forget, never take for granted, or never fail to be affected by the cross that stands as a reminder of the death of his sons and the life of the Son of God? May that be our prayer.

As I looked at the illuminated cross one dark evening, the last stanza of the hymn "Abide with Me" kept running through my mind.

> Hold Thou Thy cross before my closing eyes,
> Shine through the gloom, and point me to
>   the skies;
> Heav'n's morning breaks, and earth's vain
>   shadows flee;
> In life, in death, O Lord, abide with me.

I don't know the father whose two sons died, but I'm glad that both of us know a Father whose Son died on a cross on a hill called Calvary. What a powerful, constant memorial of life for us to keep our eyes on at all times.

Father to Father: Father, hold Your Son's cross always before me and my family. Illuminate it so its message might reflect off us. In life, in death, O Lord, abide with us. In the name and living memory of Christ Crucified I pray. Amen.

God's Man in Action: Use twigs, toothpicks, paper, or scraps of wood to create a simple cross to display in your house or office. Use it as a constant reminder of Jesus' life, death, and resurrection and its meaning in your life.

Diamonds Can Be a Man's Best Friend

Psalm 20:5

Spring training is over and the boys of summer are ready for another swing at the World Series. Growing up, I was going to be a pitcher for the St. Louis Cardinals. Now my dream is gone but I'm still hoping for a call to be the team chaplain. I've had lots of practice praying for them. When I was growing up, the baseball diamond was one of my best friends as I played Little League and watched the Cardinals.

Sitting in my desk are some box-seat tickets for a game this weekend. I love to take my children to the ball game. What a great bonding time as we throw peanut shells on the ground, yell at the top of our lungs, do the wave, and sing "Take Me Out to the Ball Game" as the home team brings home a victory.

Going to a baseball game can be a spiritual experience for me. It's fun to "see" God and learn about walking in His steps, even at the stadium. There are many similarities between our spiritual walk and a ball game. One day I shared some of these thoughts with my confirmation class. One of the students had fun adding to my list. Here's what we came up with. (Note: We won't refer to the "in the big-inning" baseball verse in Genesis 1:1.)

Both ball games and worship begin with singing. There are times when we stand and when we sit.

Satan's forces (the other team) and God's ways (the home team) are trying to win. There is much celebration (in heaven and in the stands) when the home team comes out victorious.

Sharing the experience with your family only enhances the time together. There is much to learn about faith and trust as one hands a $20 bill down an aisle of 15 people and expects both food and the proper change to return. There are times when the player/pray-er strikes out, but how thankful we are for a second chance a short time later (forgiveness). Some people like to watch (worship) from a distance and some like front-row seats.

Sometimes a substitute takes the place of someone who isn't doing well. The substitute might even make a sacrifice play—talk about a spiritual experience! There is only one way to get home—if you try another way, you're out. (Jesus is the only way home.)

All participants are important, even though they use their gifts in different ways. (A team can't play well if everyone wants to be a catcher and no one wants to play right field.) The visiting team (Satan's side) will throw curves, hoping the home team will strike out. It takes a keen focus and concentration to play the game.

Coaches (encouragers, pastors, teachers, etc.) play an important role in completing the game plan.

When the game is over, a lot of people go home. We shout for joy for the victory that is ours.

Let us lift our banners in the name of our victorious manager and Most Valuable Player—Jesus Christ!

(Baseball) diamonds can be a man's best friend, but they can also help a man see his best friend, Jesus Christ, better. It all depends on your perspective.

Father to Father: Father, it's fun to see You and Your life-giving work in all that I do. Thank You for including me on Your home team and providing me the victory through Jesus Christ. Amen.

God's Man in Action: Depending on the season and your location, take your children to a ball game. While you're there, celebrate God's victory. If a ball game isn't possible, think of interests you have and creatively tie them in with your faith walk.

A Wise Choice

James 1:5

S arah and Christopher were playing school. Five-year-old Christopher was the teacher, and his older sister was the student. Sarah started an assignment that Christopher supplied. "Teacher" was checking next week's lesson plans when he was interrupted. "I don't understand this question," Sarah said. Christopher came to her desk, looked intently at the assignment, and realized something very important. "Wait, I don't know how to read," he said.

This exchange reminded me of how often I like to play the role of teacher when the appropriate role would be that of student. Many times in my role as father I've said, "I don't know the answer and I'm not sure I even understand the question." While I've been called to be a father, I also need to remember that first of all I am a son ... of God. Although fathers teach their children, I also need to be a student under the tutelage of rabbi Jesus.

The role of father (not to mention husband, employee, employer, job seeker, coach, answer man, etc.) is an awesome responsibility. It can be overwhelming at times.

Solomon knew about being overwhelmed. He was anointed king after his father. The Lord came to Solomon in a dream and said, "Ask for whatever you want Me to give you." Standing in awe of God and overwhelmed by his calling as king, Solomon replied, "Now, O LORD my God, You have made Your servant king in place of my father David. But I am only a little child and do not know how to carry out my duties. Your servant is here among the people You have chosen, a great people, too numerous to count or number. So give Your servant a discerning heart to govern Your people and to distinguish between right and wrong" (1 Kings 3:7–9).

You know the rest of the story. God granted Solomon the requested wisdom and threw in riches and honor as a bonus, asking him to walk in His righteous ways.

How often is wisdom on your prayer list? Does it make your top 10 requests? As awesome as Solomon's kingly calling was, so is yours, as father to the children that God has entrusted to your care. Solomon saw himself as an inexperienced child. (He was probably about 20 years old.) His list of duties seemed overwhelming. He felt like a servant with a great number of responsibilities. Being an anointed father isn't all that different. One common thread ties our calling with Solomon's—the need for wisdom. And not just any wisdom or common sense will do. We don't need book knowledge or letters behind a name. What is necessary is wisdom from heaven. Godly wisdom is needed to make decisions with and for your family. Wisdom from the mind of God to yours is necessary to lead a family focused on Christ, the King. When called to distinguish between right and wrong, who doesn't need the wisdom of the one who created the heavens and the earth?

James had God's wisdom inspiring him when he wrote, "If any of you lacks wisdom, he should ask God, who gives generously to all without finding fault, and it will be given to him" (James 1:5). It seems so easy.

It is. Ask and you shall receive. Ask and keep your mind open as God pours His heavenly wisdom over your life and ways. Ask your God, who is generous with His gifts. Move wisdom up to the top of your prayer list. God's generous portion of wisdom overwhelms the concerns and fears you once had about your anointed calling as father.

Father to Father: Father, grant me wisdom for my anointed calling. In Jesus' name. Amen.

God's Man in Action: On a clock face, tape a reminder that reads, "Time to Ask for Wisdom!" Or, on your wrist, next to your watch, print a W to remind you to ask for wisdom.

Look Who's Not Talking

1 Kings 19:11–13

A brochure from the Family Initiative Council contained an astonishing statistic. It noted that fathers spend an average of 39 seconds a day talking with their children. Thirty-nine seconds!

Take 39 seconds out of your day right now to help you realize how long (or short) that time really is. I thought about some common "dad lines" such as, "Hi. How was your day? Did you do anything special? Did you wash your hands for supper? Sweet dreams. I love you. Good night." Those took 12 seconds, giving time for simple yes or no answers. That leaves 27 seconds, if you want to make the average.

The day after I read this statistic, I observed an interesting father-son lunch. I shouldn't have eavesdropped, but they were so close to me that it was difficult not to overhear and observe them. I'm guessing that the boy was 10 years old. It was obvious that father and son were uneasy with each other. After a long silence and a lot of drink sipping, the father broke the silence by describing a recent $80,000 business deal. His son raised his eyebrows but didn't seem sincerely interested. Searching for conversation topics, the father blurted out, "I should check my messages. Okay?" The son nodded.

The father checked his pockets and then asked his son, "Do you have a quarter?" The response was negative so the father trekked off towards the cashier. By the time the father returned, their orders were ready. This seemed like a welcome relief for both since they shouldn't talk with their mouths full. Between bites the father did ask, "Is it good?" He received an "uh huh" in return. The son then said he was cold and would be waiting outside in the sun while his father finished eating and checked his appointment organizer.

I ask forgiveness for judging this relationship, but it seemed to me that these two had the makings of a 39-second-a-day father-son team. I hope I'm wrong.

As astonished as I was by this statistic, there have been days when it accurately described the extent of my conversations with my children. I don't like admitting that. If my children received 39 seconds of my words, what about my wife? What about God? I'm glad it's not a normal occurrence, but it's still bothersome.

Some fathers have difficulty knowing what to say to their children. Others try too hard, which is obvious to children. You don't have to talk constantly when you're spending time together. Just wanting to be with your kids speaks volumes. Don't look down on them—look up to them as God's dearly loved children. If you are struggling in this area, start simply and don't make it more difficult than it is. Discuss your children's interests, dislikes, and fears. Take turns choosing radio stations while driving in the car. Ask for their thoughts on worship styles.

If you have difficulty talking with your children, tell your heavenly Father. He speaks in thunderous ways, with gentle whispers, and through earthly dads. Discuss with Him the incredible cloud formations He created for you yesterday. Read and talk about the letters He writes you daily. Ask His advice regarding tomorrow's plans or next summer's vacation. He loves to listen and talk with His children. All the while the Expert Communicator is teaching inspired communication skills.

If 39 seconds is the average, let's strive to become above average fathers with God's help and example. Our children are worth it and need it.

Father to Father: God of second opportunities, here I am ... again! (Continue talking to your Father about His children and yours for more than 39 seconds.) Amen.

God's Man in Action: For three days note how much time you spend talking with your children. Discuss their favorite books, colors, songs, classes, friends, etc.

History Repeats Itself

Psalm 96:1–3

I presently serve as pastor of the congregation where I grew up. The baptismal font where I baptize others is the same one where I was reborn through water and the Word. The altar where I confirmed my faith in the Triune God and first received the Lord's Supper is the one where I now serve others. I grew in my faith through the blessings of the same Sunday school and Christian elementary school where my children are now learning and growing. We are all living witnesses of the truthful statement that "His-story"—Christ's story—repeats itself constantly in our lives.

Open any page of Scripture and you will find evidence of the unconditional love of God. Examples of God's undeserved love, forgiveness, and compassion fill every page of our lives as we live Christ's story—"His-story"—empowered by His Word and sacraments.

The story of God's incarnation at Christmas is repeated as your child listens to the story of Jesus' birth; when you witness the miracle of birth; or when your child gives the gift of time to the Christ child. Through it all, "His-story" repeats itself.

God's miracles are repeated with every beat of your child's heart or blink of her eye. Jesus' humanity repeats itself every time your family laughs, cries, or is hungry. The story of His deity repeats itself when you see new life in His creation, hope in a negative situation, or when Christ buries your sins and raises you to newness of life through forgiveness.

Christ's Easter story is witnessed when you face the death of a loved one and come through it with new vision; when a friendship is resurrected; when morning breaks and your household rises to face the new day He has created; when you eat and drink His body and blood given for you in the Lord's Supper for the forgiveness of sins.

"His-story" repeats itself constantly through the days God has entrusted to your care. Don't miss the daily miracles coming to you. His story is worth repeating throughout all generations.

Father to Father: Father God, what a joy it is to see Your Son's story being repeated within my family! Send Your Spirit as we continue to learn from "His-story." Amen.

God's Man in Action: Write "His-story book" on a piece of masking tape. Place it on your Bible reminding you that this is His (Christ's) story. Look for ways it repeats itself as you read and study it.

Do It All!

1 Corinthians 10:31

The world seems to scream at us to do it all. The male ego adds its own voice to the screaming crowd. We want our family to have the best. That means we have to work overtime and win the boss' favor. We want our wife to be proud, so we go overboard to win her approval. We want to be involved in all our childrens' activities, both organized and backyard fun.

Speaking of yards, we want to win the neighborhood blue ribbon for the best-groomed lot or most-improved apartment in the complex. Friendships need time and attention. The neighbors will think we're snobs if we don't invite them to a barbecue. The budget and bills need review and payment.

The church bulletin calls for board members, committee people, and volunteers. The Spirit seems to be moving us to "Do it all!" Physical self-improvement is the thing to do. The gym bag is packed and by the door. Intellectual stimulation and knowledge is important so we check out magazines, newspapers, and the local news. I didn't even mention taking time for meals.

Then it's time for bed so we can rest up for another

day of doing it all.

Men love to walk around the house with shirts off, passing every mirror to get a glimpse of the large *S* on their chest. The initial stands for a variety of titles: Superdad, Superhusband, Superservant, Superemployee, Superfriend, Supergroundskeeper, Superspiritual, and Superman. I don't know about you but just reading that list of goals wears me out.

The world and the male ego seem to urge us to try to do it all and be it all. But the Creator of our lives, bodies, families, and time never says that. He does say something very important about out efforts to do it all. He inspired Paul to write, "So whether you eat or drink or whatever you do, do it all for the glory of God" (1 Corinthians 10:31).

Obviously many men have been using the Attila the Hun translation of the Bible for this verse. Guess what fellow fathers? It doesn't say we have to *do it all.* Read it again. *Whatever* you do, do it all *for the glory of God.*

God indeed deserves all the glory. Without Him we would be nothing. We have life, breath, and being because of our God. What pure joy it is to live for Him! We can glory in giving Him the glory in all that we do and all we have become. Without Him, what do we have?

What will you be doing in the next 24 hours? Eating. Talking. Working. Planning. Thinking. Praying. Watching. Driving. Walking. Playing. Reading. Worshiping. Working out. Studying the Bible. Laughing. Leading.

Following. Volunteering. Shopping. Listening. Snacking. Banking. Writing. Caring. Hugging. Sleeping.

Whatever you do in the next 24 hours (and for the rest of your life), do it all *for the glory of God.* To God alone be the glory!

Father to Father: Father, Your Son, Jesus, did everything for Your glory. Make me aware of how I use the time You give. Also make me more alert to do everything for Your glory. Without You, where would I be? I love You, Father. Continue to make me a father after Your own heart. In Jesus' name. Amen.

God's Man in Action: Keep notes around your office, car, and home that read, "4GG" or "Do It ALL—4GG." (4GG reminds you to do it "For God's Glory.")

My Daughter—The Institution

Jeremiah 29:11

Somewhere between a bite of mashed potatoes and a gulp of milk, our daughter decided to inform us of her future plans, "When I grow up, I want to be a hospital."

My daughter wants to be an institution. What can I say, she aims high! I realized that I should probably have a talk with her regarding this lofty goal in life. I can almost envision our conversation.

Daddy: Sarah, I want you to know that I think it's great to have high expectations. In fact, God's Word says that we can do all things *through Christ,* who strengthens us.

Sarah: I know that, Daddy.

Daddy: Since you aim high, there are some things you should know. First, when you make a decision about your future, always ask God to help you make that decision. He wants and knows what's best for you. Pray that you would do what He wants—even if He wants to make you an institution.

Sarah: What's an institution?

Daddy: Well, it's like a … a hospital. Anyway, I also want you to know that whatever God wants you to be is wonderful, whether it's an institution or an inspiration. But don't worry about your future—let God be in charge of your plans. I know He has great plans for you. Worrying about it only tells God we don't trust Him.

Sarah: I'm not worried, Daddy.

Daddy: No matter what you are when you grow up, you will be important in God's eyes and in the eyes and hearts of your mother and me. We will always love you. But if God does bless you by making you an institution, I hope you will stay humble, like Jesus. The Bible says to brag about Jesus, not ourselves. Without Him we can do nothing. There is one other thing. When you try things, sometimes you will fail. Don't panic! You can learn from your failures. Just keep trying and counting on Jesus' help. He kept going toward His goal—the cross— even though things got rough.

Sarah: Hey, is this one of your sermons?

Daddy: I don't think so. (*Pause*) Sarah, if you want to be a hospital and if God wants you to be an institution, that's wonderful. If God brings it about, He will bless you and help you achieve whatever goals you and He decide on.

Sarah: That's great, Daddy, but I didn't mean I wanted to *be* a hospital. I meant I wanted to work in a hospital—like a nurse or doctor. Can I please go out and play now?

Daddy: So you don't actually want to be a hospital? (*Sarah shakes her head.*) Well, I guess you can go out and play. But Sarah, you might want to remember this little talk as you make more and more decisions in life.

Sarah: Dad, I'm only 4 years old! (*Running out the door*) Bye, Daddy. (*Running back in*) I love you bunches!

Daddy: I love you too, Sarah! By the way, what are you going to play?

Sarah: Nurse and doctor.

Daddy: I think we should have another talk tomorrow.

Sarah has recently changed her mind and plans to be a school—I mean a teacher.

Father to Father: Pray that God's plans will be accomplished in the lives of your family members.

God's Man in Action: Ask your children what they have thought of doing when they grow up. This may be a good time to encourage them to consider full-time church careers. Encourage them in their ideas, even if they include "institutional" work.

Spare Me Change

Malachi 3:6

The saying goes that the only person who likes change is a baby with a dirty diaper. Everyone deals with change differently. Change in our lives often affects others, so a person not only deals with the change but how those around him respond.

Some changes are daily irritations but are easy to handle. But many changes, especially those that catch us off guard, seem to turn our world upside down. When changes surprise us, what a blessing it is to trust and live in the promises of our God. If you find change unsettling, settle comfortably into the truth that your Father says, "I the LORD do not change." God is always faithful to His Word.

Noah found God flooding his family with faithfulness to His Word despite the storms of life. The Lord was faithful to His promise to see Abram and Sarai through a family move as well as the change that a baby would bring them, even in their old age. God kept a 430-year promise of freedom to His people in Egypt's captivity. He followed that with a Promised Land promise.

Has anyone endured more drastic changes and trusted in the changeless God more than Job? Hosea was called to trust in God, who saw him through the changes and difficulties of a marriage to a less than godly woman. Mary and Joseph were carried safely by God through incredible changes, as well as through the teenage years of Jesus and their other children. Saul not only underwent a name change but numerous life changes under God's constant protection.

As changes affect our family, we trust in a change-less God who says one day we will all be changed—in a flash, in the twinkling of an eye—at the last trumpet. That final change, when Christ returns, will be our last and most glorious change. We will be clothed with the imperishable, and we will never face change again.

That final change will happen because of a change that happened in the life of Jesus. The God of the universe, the Creator of all creation, the one who can destroy a city with a word or create faith through water and His Word, came down from heaven to dwell among us. The Word—the Christ—became flesh and blood so that we who live in a changing, sinful world might be changed to be like Him. Christ put on flesh and walked among us, teaching us to trust His Father, our Father. He took on human form, and the changes that life and death bring us, so that we would know the change that comes through faith in Him. It is a change that gives us hope and peace through His gift of life.

Not all change is bad. God's Spirit, working through His Word, is bringing many positive changes into the lives of His people. Following Christ is a call to change toward His perfect will and away from our sinful ways. God is also a master at using changes in our lives that we view as negative for His glory and our good.

If change in our lives brings undue stress and pressures, we need to turn to our changeless God and ask Him to increase our trust in His promises to see us safely through.

Father to Father: Change me, changeless Father, to trust You through the many changes of my life. Where You see need for change in my life, grant me Your power and Spirit to bring it about for Your glory. I bring these requests to You through Your Son. Amen.

God's Man in Action: When you handle change (coins) today, rejoice in God's changeless love and ways. Pray that He will work positive changes in your life.

A Question of Love

Proverbs 3:11–12

Take one minute to consider how you have shown love to your children this week. How many did you think of? Your list may include a hug, an "I love you," working to be able to provide for them, a kiss, taking them to church, helping with homework, discipline ... Anyone consider discipline a way to show love? Anyone besides God, that is? The Bible certainly emphasizes the importance of discipline, motivated by love, as part of caring for our children. I realize this is a sensitive issue today, when any type of discipline is considered child abuse by someone.

Just as we would stand up for any part of Scripture, I think we need to say that properly motivated, appropriate discipline shows love for our children. There is no doubt that we also have too many inappropriate, sinful actions disguised as discipline. But we aren't loving our children when we allow them to do anything.

Just as speaking the truth in love is a healthy gift from God for relationships, discipline in love is part of Godly fathering.

Let's take a moment to search Scripture on this subject. Most of the words are found, interestingly enough, in a book of wisdom.

- Proverbs 3:11–12 reads: "My son, do not despise the Lord's discipline and do not resent His rebuke, because the Lord disciplines those He loves, as a father the son he delights in."
- In Proverbs 13:24, we find these words: "He who spares the rod hates his son, but he who loves him is careful to discipline him." (*Rod* is likely a figure of speech representing any type of discipline.)
- Proverbs 19:18 tells us: "Discipline your son, for in that there is hope."
- Proverbs 29:15 reads: "The rod of correction imparts wisdom, but a child left to himself disgraces his mother."

There are also many passages that point to God's wisdom and love as He disciplines us, His children whom He loves. A portion of Hebrews addresses this matter.

Endure hardship as discipline; God is treating you as sons. For what son is not disciplined by his father? If you are not disciplined ... then you are illegitimate children. ... We have all had human fathers who disciplined us and we respected them for it. ... Our fathers disciplined us for a little while as they thought best; but God disciplines us for our good, that we may share in

His holiness. No discipline seems pleasant
at the time, but painful. Later on, however,
it produces a harvest of righteousness and
peace for those who have been trained by it.
(Hebrews 12:7–10)

God's Word is clear on this subject that many people
are uncomfortable discussing. Fathers, in love—and
only in love—wisely discipline your children. But,
fathers, do not misuse these passages in a way that is
not God-pleasing.

Before disciplining, examine your motive. If you are
disciplining purely out of anger, then go no farther. If
your discipline is motivated by outside forces (frustration at work, guilt, headaches, etc.) then stop. Also,
remember to make punishments equal to the misdeed.

Now that I am an adult, I am thankful for the wise
discipline I received. Although I wanted a free reign,
the loving discipline I received was grounded in God's
Word. (Maybe "grounded" is bad word choice.)

Father to Father: Father, today Your Word reminded me
that You discipline because You love me and want what is
best for me. Continually help me to love and discipline as
You do. In the name of Jesus I pray. Amen.

God's Man in Action: Consider any discipline you may
have given this week. If it was not motivated by love, ask
your children for forgiveness.

A Casting Call

1 Peter 5:7

O nce a father who loved to fish tried to teach me some practical theology. (Any father who deals with pressures, problems, and anxieties may want to sit in on this lesson.) At first I was lured into his way of thinking. He put the bait on, and I went for it hook, line, and sinker—until I examined the catch and realized it should be thrown back.

The seemingly helpful hint this fisherman cast to me one day was in reference to 1 Peter 5:7, "Cast all your anxiety on Him because He cares for you." This father who was hooked on fishing told me that he just puts all his problems on the hook, flexes his elbow, winds up, and casts them out to Jesus. Interesting concept.

I couldn't wait to try it out. Anxieties weren't hard to find and there is always time for prayer. So as I prayed, I envisioned myself "casting" my cares out to Jesus, who cares for me. About an hour later I found that the anxieties I had just cast out to my Savior had resurfaced in my life. I cast them out again. Later I found myself dealing with the same old problems and concerns I thought I had cast away.

What's wrong with this picture? I don't have much

fishing experience but I soon realized why this catch of the day was going to have to be thrown back.

Picture yourself fishing. Weigh down your hook with the wiggling, anxious worm. Then cast. What happens next? After sitting peacefully for awhile, you find yourself reeling the line back in, and before long, you are looking that worm in the eye again. It's back!

I can't tell you how many times I thought I had cast all my cares on Christ only to find them looking at me moments later. It's hard to cut the line and let go.

So I turned to another fisherman for advice. This fisherman knew about anxieties. He knew about fishing. And he knew about casting. His name is Peter. He was the fisherman who once caught more fish than his nets could handle. He won't deny that he learned about casting his anxieties after he denied his Lord. He learned about practical theology when he began fishing for men as well as for fish. This fisherman made many wonderful, Spirit-led discoveries about living the Christian life. I trust you are familiar with this fisherman. He penned the inspired words, "Cast all your anxieties on Him [Jesus] because He cares for you."

I need to point out that Peter wasn't writing about casting a fishing net or line. Those we pull back in. Originally, the meaning of his words was to cast or throw upon something or, in this case, upon someone—Jesus Christ. A more appropriate picture is carrying a large rock and casting it, throwing it away, from ourselves. We won't be reeling back a large rock.

Go ahead! Let go! Throw all your cares and anxieties. Don't cast them and reel them back in. Throw them on Christ because He does care deeply about every aspect of your life. Cast away as God's Word calls us to do. Then you can fish in peace—for fish and for people.

What's right with this picture? Everything!

Father to Father: Thank You for Your call to cast all my anxieties on You. Help me let go of them, giving them to Jesus. What a gracious Friend and Savior! Amen.

God's Man in Action: Carry a fishing weight in your pocket this week. Let it remind you of God's casting call.

Pray Now, Pray Later

Philippians 4:6

Immediately following tonight's evening newscast, stay tuned for ... prayer! Prayer following the news. It seems like a natural response to hearing news from the scene of a sin-filled, hurting, hating, and violent world. Often, after hearing horrifying news, my wife and I share concerns for our children growing up in the middle of a world that seems to grow more hateful by the hour.

These conversations of concern also can be sparked by a talk show in which children are grossly disrespectful to their parents. They can start after overhearing a conversation in a parking lot regarding domestic violence in someone's home. Or the subject may come up after reading astonishing statistics about the immorality of this society.

I imagine similar conversations have been shared in your home. What will the world be like when our children go to college, get married, or try to follow Christ in a world that mocks His Word? Negativity and fear are not my goals in sharing these thoughts with you. But it seems to be a realistic concern for Christian parents.

We spend our lives trying to protect our children.

It's difficult to realize we aren't able to protect them from all ungodly things. Our concerns especially grow out of a great respect for their most precious gift—their faith in God. The one thing Satan would have us believe is that there is nothing we can do about our children's future. Don't let him hang that falsehood on the latch of your children's hope chest!

We can begin by being faithful to our own calling as Christian parents. Let's surround our children with God's truth in a world of falsehoods. Let's remind them constantly of God's promise to walk with us through the difficulties of life. We shouldn't try to hide the truths of living in a sinful world—not any more than we should hide the truths of living as God's dearly loved children. We need to teach them of God's forgiveness through the forgiveness in which we, ourselves, live daily. We can live in the joyful state of trusting God.

One of the greatest gifts we can give our children is our prayers. Pray now; pray later. Pray now for their future spouse—if marriage is part of God's plan for them. Pray that the Lord would build up the faith of the people they will date. Pray now that their God-given talents be developed so they will glorify God in their future work. Pray now for gifts of self-control and love. Pray now that your relationship will be a God-glorifying example for their future relationships. Pray daily that God will guard their faith when it is attacked. Pray now for His angels to protect them from Satan's deadly arrows. Pray that God will use your faith today to affect their tomorrows. Pray now; pray later. Keep the prayers ascending to heaven and rejoice as God's grace, love, and protection descend on them.

Your children's lives won't be without hurts, pain, or even death. But God's promise is that He will not leave them or forsake them (or their parents). As our prayers ascend, we find that God is not only strengthening their faith, but ours as well. Even through the difficult times, we rejoice that our faith is mature and strong, helping to point our children to our God of hope.

Pray now. Pray later. Pray. And the peace of God will guard your hearts and minds in Christ Jesus.

Father to Father: Pray now, bombarding God's throne of grace with petitions for your children—for today and for all their tomorrows.

God's Man in Action: Jesus prayed for future generations of believers just before He died. Read Jesus' petitions for each of us in John 17 (especially verses 20–26). Make a list of your prayer requests for your children's future. Make an extra copy and put it in their baby books. When they are grown, they will have a witness of your prayers and God's answers.

Labor Day Remembered

Isaiah 9:6

D o you remember the thoughts that flooded your mind when your wife told you she was going into labor?

- This is really happening. We're going to have a baby. We really are!

- I forgot everything from the Lamaze class! I must remember something about coaching. Let's see: "Hey, batter, batter, batter! Swing!" Wrong sport. Think she'll notice?

- What if I have to deliver the baby in the car?

- This is my wife, and we need a room *now!* Forget everyone else ... please?

- I wonder what labor pains feel like? This probably isn't a good time to ask.

- God, help! Please, let everything go smoothly. Keep the baby safe. Help my wife. (And I wouldn't mind a little help either.) Please, God!

- What is this? An interns' field trip to our birth room? Come on, this is a private moment. It looks as though all modesty goes flying out the window when giving birth.

- Back labor! Breathe. Breathe. I'm so nervous. Breathe.

- Look ... her heartbeat! Or his heartbeat. What a beautiful, incredible sight! There are three heartbeats in this room. I can't wait to see the face that goes with that one.

- This is taking longer than I thought.

- Why is my wife yelling at me? I didn't do anything. I just told her how much I love her. Wow! Motherhood brings many changes.

- I've got this down. She's cold—pull up covers. A contraction is coming according to the monitor. Get into position. Fist under her back—rub in circles. Coach her breathing. Follow the pain through. Now she's hot—put cloth on her head, pull down covers. Wait.

- I am so in awe of her. I had no idea she had this stamina and strength. There's something divine going on. She's incredible!

- I wish I could take her place for a while— give her a break (I think).

- What's going on in the next room? The yelling doesn't help the morale in here.

- It's getting close now. Please, God, stay near. Keep us all safe.

- Bear down, honey. I hate seeing her in pain. Push! Keep on? Give her a break, doc. She can't take it. God, give her the strength she needs *now* ... please?

- Ah, the top of the head. *Our* baby's head!

- Push one more time! Push, honey! The shoulders ... Our baby!

- It's a boy? Are you sure? I thought for sure it would be a girl. A boy, huh? We have a son! It's a miracle—a gift from God.

- I'm a dad! Honey, we have a baby. He's beautiful and so tiny.

- Me? Cut the cord? I don't think ... okay. I cut my son's umbilical cord—cool!

- Listen ... crying—baby, Mom, and Dad.

- That's the most beautiful sight I've ever seen: mother and child.

- Thank You, God! Unto us a child is born—a heaven-sent miracle wrapped in Your grace and my wife's arms. Protect this child from this day on. Help me be the kind of dad You want me to be. Thank You, God. It was the most miraculous thing I have ever witnessed. The miracle of life—Your miracle of life, God. I'm honored. I'm nervous. I'm a dad!

Father to Father: Miracle Worker, cause me to appreciate the miracles that live in my house. You are awesome. Your miracles are awesome, simply awesome. Amen.

God's Man in Action: Reminisce about the thoughts and events surrounding your children's births. Every time you pass a hospital or a baby this week, offer a prayer.

Firmed in Christ

Hebrews 4:14

It was Sunday morning and our daughter was confused. We were driving in the opposite direction from church. Sarah finally spoke up. "Why aren't we going to our church? Where are we going?"

Her big brother supplied the answer. "We are going to Sondra's church. Today Sondra is getting firmed." As my wife and I tried to suppress our amusement, I realized that he was right, even if he wasn't correct! Sondra was our neighbor, and she was getting confirmed. She would make a public profession of her faith and receive the Lord's Supper. So Benjamin was correct. Sondra was confirming her faith, and she was getting "firmed" in Christ.

Sondra was a special young lady. For years she had been sitting firmly in a wheelchair because of the disabling disease muscular dystrophy. Today she would confirm her faith in her Triune God who was "firming" her faith through His vehicles of grace.

About a year later, I learned that God had confirmed His promise of heaven to Sondra, whose faith He had been firming up daily. Sondra left her wheelchair and now worships at the altar of God's heavenly throne.

What a blessing Sondra received in God's gift of

Christian parents who knew the importance of being firmed in Christ. What a blessing Sondra received in a church that gracefully shared God's firming gifts of Word and sacraments. What a gift Sondra received when God raised her to a new and eternal life through the waters of Baptism.

The writer of Hebrews reminds God's people: "Let us hold firmly to the faith we profess." What an important word for all of us who suffer from the disability of sinfulness and its accompanying curse of death. Our sin disease cripples us, but the Great Physician of body and soul has the medicine that helps us stand firm and strong. His Word and sacraments keep us firmed in Christ for this life and beyond.

Where are you going today? God wants you to journey to His altar, with your family, to be firmed in Christ.

Father to Father: Father, thank You for the daily opportunities You give me to be firmed in Christ. In the firm name of Jesus. Amen.

God's Man in Action: Write the words of Hebrews 4:14 on a strip of masking tape. Place the message on something that you grab hold of during your day (a door handle, steering wheel, exercise machine grip). Let it be a reminder to hold firmly to the faith you profess.

A Toast to You

Matthew 26:27

I've witnessed many toasts at wedding receptions, anniversary parties, and other celebrations. But I can't recall seeing a father toast his family. There have been friends toasting friends, siblings sharing a toast, spouses lifting a glass in honor of the other. But father to family I don't remember witnessing.

Toasting didn't mean all that much to me until I attended a reception where the best man explained how the practice came about. He shared that centuries ago, many alcoholic beverages were made through a process that involved lead tubing or pipes. As the drink was processed, lead particles would end up in the drink. The lead in drinks could cause illness or eventual death to those who drank them.

As a sign of caring, a host would offer each guest a small piece of toast, placing it in their drinks. The bread would absorb the foreign, potentially deadly particles. Once removed, guests could drink in celebration. To give someone a toast was a sign of great love and loyalty.

With this explanation in mind, it seems appropriate for fathers to lift their cups (of chocolate milk, water, or juice) in a toast to their families. Isn't it our prayer that God would use us in removing harmful things from our family's path? Wouldn't it be great to actually absorb our children's fears, hurts, and concerns so they wouldn't have to handle them alone?

Although we can't take away all our loved one's concerns, we can—with God's help—remove some dangerous obstacles. That may mean a change in our lifestyle, words, or habits that could be potentially dangerous to them. It may call for getting to know our children better so we can help them with their problems. Becoming more aware of harmful traps around our family members is an important step in purifying our family's cup. One thing we can't remove is the poison of sin. That takes a toast from our brother Jesus.

On the night before He was crucified, at a type of rehearsal for a wedding feast, Jesus lifted a cup to His friends. In essence, He said to them, "I toast you, My friends! Take eat. Take drink. This is My body and blood shed for you for the forgiveness of all your sins." On the cross, Jesus absorbed all of our poisonous, deadly sins into His body. His Father did not remove the cup of suffering from His life; rather, He caused His Son to raise the cup in a toast like no other—to give His life for us. In return the Father gave *us* forgiveness, life, and peace. In raising the cup of salvation, Jesus raises us to new heights as His honored, forgiven brothers and sisters.

Let's take steps to purify our homes, cleansed in the

blood of Jesus. Let's also take our Savior's example and honor our family members with a toast at breakfast, lunch, or supper. Every day and every life is a reason to celebrate God's grace and His gift of family.

Father to Father: Father, You have honored us by lifting Your cup of salvation and toasting us through Your Son's suffering, death, and resurrection. We honor Your name and gifts by purifying our homes and honoring one another as Your dearly loved children. In the name of Jesus we pray and live. Amen.

God's Man in Action: Whatever the cups at the next meal hold, honor your family members by giving them a toast, along with a taste of your great love and respect for them.

The Inside Story

Matthew 23:25–26

Benjamin's third-grade class was making a cookbook to raise money for a playground. All the parents received a note from the teacher asking for favorite recipes. Benjamin and my wife picked out some of their favorites to add to this volume.

I didn't want to be left out so I turned in my own. They included such culinary delights as:

- Potato Chip Salad—Mix three different brands of potato chips in a large bowl. Chill and serve.

- Elephant Stew—Combine one medium elephant, salt and pepper to taste, and two rabbits. (Rabbits optional because most people don't like to find "hares" in their stew.)

- The Time-Honored Wesemann Family Peanut Butter and Jelly Sandwich—Spread 2½ teaspoons of peanut butter (creamy, not chunky) on one slice of bread. Spread 2½ teaspoons of grape jam on another slice of bread. Place the bread slices together. (Note: When combining bread slices, the ingredients should be on the inside.)

Parents spend lots of time making themselves and their children look great on the outside. That includes having the coolest hairstyles, the latest fashions, the best manners, the whitest and straightest teeth, or stunning makeup. There is nothing wrong with any of these by themselves, but what's really important is what's on the inside.

When a peanut butter and jelly sandwich has the ingredients on the outside, we end up with a mess on our hands that is hard to swallow. The same sandwich with the ingredients on the inside becomes a great tasting, hunger-satisfying meal.

On the outside the Pharisees looked like the most upright, God-fearing people in the community. But Jesus could tell that the ingredients were all on the outside. There was little coming from their hearts. Jesus paints a powerful picture with His words as He tells the Pharisees that they wash the outside of the cup and dish but are full of greed and self-indulgence inside. He tells them to first clean the inside of the dish, and then the outside also will be clean (Matthew 23:25–26).

Examine your life and the lives of your children, which you are shaping. Are both the inside and outside clean? Is Christ, who lives within you, showing on the outside?

We can quote whole chapters of the Bible by heart, but if the message is not in our heart, it can be difficult for people to swallow the life-saving message. If we can call hymns or liturgical phrases to mind but are not transformed by the renewing of our mind in Christ (Romans 12:2), we just have a mess on our hands. If we look good on the outside but out of our hearts comes evil thoughts and actions (Matthew 15:19), our hunger for life is never satisfied.

As Christian parents, we need to be concerned about the inside and outside of our lives and our children's lives.Others may not know what's going on inside your life right now. You may be able to fool some people, but you can't fool God. Gracefully swallow the forgiveness that the Bread of Life offers. He wants to live within you and satisfy your hunger for an abundant, forgiven, and eternal life.

Christ living within us is the best recipe for life. Taste and see that the Lord is good.

Father to Father: Father, send Jesus to live within me. He is the ingredient I need to have a fulfilling and eternal life. Forgive the mess that I have on my hands and heart. Cleanse me and feed me with Your Words of life. In my Savior's name I pray. Amen.

God's Man in Action: In the mood for a peanut butter and jelly sandwich? Make one (remember—ingredients on the inside). As you eat, meditate on 2 Corinthians 4:13–18 and 1 Corinthians 13. Then wash it down with 1 Peter 2:1–3.

Known by His Works

John 6:27 and Romans 7:18, 24–25

O ne evening our family of four (at that time) took turns sharing what we thought each person was good at doing. We wanted to encourage one another in the gifts God had entrusted to us.

I shared with Benjamin that he was a good artist. He has been blessed with many talents, one of which is an artistic, creative gift. Then I shared with Sarah that she was a very good singer. She loved to sing the songs she was learning in Sunday school and preschool. I shared with my wife that she was very gifted at being a great mom and all that entailed.

When it came time for them to share what I was good at, I wished I had never started this exercise in encouragement. With great boldness and painstaking honesty, Benjamin told me that I was good at two things. One was work. The other was throwing things on the floor next to my bed. *Ouch!*

When Benjamin mentioned that I was good at work, I don't think he meant that I was good at carrying out God's ministry or being a good preacher. I'm sure he meant I was good at work because it took up so much of my time … and then the messy floor comment. I work too much and I'm a slob! If this was our encouragement time, I think I'll skip next week's family session on speaking the truth in love. They already had that mastered.

It is good to spend some time in the reality chair, which is not to be confused with the easy chair. Obviously, full-time ministry requires a lot of time. But so does our full-time calling to dadhood and husbandhood. Benjamin was correct. At that time I was spending too much time at work and not enough time working on my other divine callings. It seems odd, but I had put work—which was God's work—before God and family. I needed that wake-up call. In my son's eyes, I was known for my work. I hope he wouldn't answer in the same manner today. (I think I will ask for an updated answer this week.)

When I hear those kinds of remarks from my family, I can rejoice that Jesus is known by His work … on the cross. When my priorities get out of whack, I pray that God will use His Word, His people, or any other means to show me my sin. I also pray that God will immediately send me to His workplace. Jesus Christ worked salvation and forgiveness for all my sins at the place of the skull—Golgotha. But I also find Him exiting His workplace, when His work was finished, through a darkened tomb once sealed shut. As I walk with Him, I realize that this is my God who has not only won the victory over sin for me but also has the power to help me change from my sinful ways as He works within my life.

I pray that I am becoming better at working ... working at allowing God's truth to penetrate everything I do in this life. What a blessing to see God at work through my son's candor. It ended as an evening of encouragement after all, thanks to the unseen Guest who was behind the scenes, leading our discussion.

In regard to the pile of things next to my bed, well, let's just say I'm getting worse at being good at that.

Father to Father: Father, sometimes I put work before You and my family. I want to always praise You with the gifts and talents You have entrusted to my care. Help me work at my relationship with You as You align my ways with Your will. Thank You for Your life-saving work through Jesus, my Savior. Amen.

God's Man in Action: Take time this week, as a family, to celebrate the gifts God has entrusted to each individual. Don't forget to thank the unseen Guest for what He is good at doing in your lives.

Ageless Children

1 John 3:1

When I was a junior in high school, I remember a question the teacher posed to our class. I thought it was a very odd question but an easy one to answer. Without much thought, my classmates and I quickly jotted our answers on paper. The teacher had asked us, "If you could be one age for the rest of your life, what age would you choose?" You can imagine the answers from a class full of teenagers. There were two frequently noted ages—18 and 21.

There was one answer that stood out. My friend said that if he could choose, he would like to be 3 years old. We couldn't believe his response! Who wants to be 3? When you're 21, you can do whatever you want. You can get married, make lots of money (or so we thought), buy a car, and you don't have to live at home.

My friend calmly explained his reasoning. A 3-year-old doesn't have to worry about dating, school, marital problems, taxes, car payments, job stress, or appearance. As a 3-year-old he would be loved unconditionally, pampered, fed, housed, taken care of, and also lovingly disciplined. He could play most of the day, take afternoon naps, eat peanut butter and jelly sandwiches without worrying about calories or cholesterol, rely on parents for help and guidance in most every decision, and basically have very few cares in the world.

His answer makes sense now that I'm not a 16-year-old. Have you ever wanted to change ages and places with your young child? Obviously, we don't have that option. Physically, it's impossible—spiritually, it's not.

Spiritually, I have seen some very mature 3-year-olds. I mean that in a scriptural sense, in a most complimentary way. Jesus said, "Unless you change and become like little children, you will never enter the kingdom of heaven" (Matthew 18:3). And on another occasion He said, "Anyone who will not receive the kingdom of God like a little child will never enter it" (Mark 10:15).

Scripture also teaches us that we must grow in our faith, to mature, not letting the seed of faith die. The more mature we become in our faith, the more we become like a younger and younger child. What a gift to have a faith that is totally trusting and unpretentious! Children of God who are mature in their faith realize that they are helpless when it comes to entering the kingdom of God; they must rely totally on the unconditional, undeserved love of their Father, through Jesus Christ.

You are a child of God—act like one. Trust—don't worry. Enjoy—don't fret. Rely on God's strength and wisdom—not your own. Put away bitterness—put on smiles. Pray what's in your heart. Love unconditionally. Don't keep the hurts and anger bottled up inside— run to your Father. Look forward to going to church and Sunday school. Color God's world full of bright colors. Sing out His praise, whether on key or off.

In your faith walk, strive to be a very mature 3-year-old Christian. It's not a step backwards. It's a step within the Father's footstep that leads forever forward.

Go ahead, grab the peanut butter and jelly and crawl up in the lap of your Lord with a good book—the Bible. Go on a childhood adventure that will never end. Enjoy and grow in this day that He has made especially for you, His precious child.

Father to Father: It's me, Father, Your child. Forgive me for trying to be such an adult in my faith when You call me to enjoy a mature childlike faith. Help me to trust, live, worship, enjoy, love, and be loved like a child—Your child. I love You, Father God. In Jesus' name. Amen.

God's Man in Action: Whether with your children or alone, sing some favorite childhood "Jesus songs."

We're Hungry—Say Grace

2 Corinthians 12:7–9

I imagine that it happens around every family table. It's usually accompanied by preteen giggles and middle-age sneers. The scene is set as stomachs growl. The clock closes in on evening activities. The cook has worn a path between the stove, the sink, and the refrigerator. The patience level is low. The anxiety level is high.

Then the grumbling starts to quake: "How long? We're hungry! I've got to leave in a few minutes!" Finally everyone is seated. "Would someone say grace?" You know what comes next—"Grace!" shouts son number 1. With that, hands grab, faces are fed, and hunger is immediately satisfied.

You've been surrounded by a chorus of growling stomachs waiting for "grace" so you can have your fill. But you also have been surrounded by other hunger pains. There have been times when you are hungry for answers to tough decisions, starved for attention, famished for relief from the pain, looking for a break from the pressure, hungry for compassion or guidance.

We have been there. Paul has also been there. He was hungry. But before having his hunger satisfied, "grace" was spoken—by the Lord Himself. Immediately Paul's hunger was satisfied.

Paul tells the Corinthians about a thorn in his flesh. It seems to be some physical pain or disability that constantly tortured him. The word *thorn* can be translated in a variety of ways. It can describe a stake used for impaling or torturing someone, a sharpened wooden staff, a thorn, or a splinter. Whatever was torturing him, Paul was hungry for relief and help. The Lord knew his hunger and heard his repetitive pleas so He said "grace."

The Lord told Paul, "My grace is sufficient for you, for My power is made perfect in weakness." With that, Paul's hunger was satisfied. Take note of the change that follows. Paul began to delight in weaknesses, insults, hardships, and persecution. He realized that when he was weak, he was strong. The Lord gently removed the cotton that Satan placed in Paul's ears when he had his mind on his flesh. The Lord came close and whispered in his ear, "Grace, Paul. My grace. It is sufficient!" Paul tasted and trusted in the truth of God's nourishing Word.

Hungry? Before your hunger is satisfied, make sure grace is said. Allow the unseen Guest at your table to say "grace." It will be sufficient.

Then hang on for the ride that follows. God's grace can turn your world upside down. But what a great view! You might find yourself rejoicing while the rest of the world is moaning. You may start loving things that everyone else hates. You will find yourself boasting in the Lord rather than in yourself.

The hunger pains are flaring up again. We're hungry. Would someone please say grace? In the fullness of time, Son number 1 stretched out His hands rather than folding them. He did not close His eyes, rather, He eyed heaven. From the cross He cried out loudly, "Grace!" With that, our hunger was completely satisfied. His grace is sufficient.

Father to Father: Lord, I'm hungry. Say grace. It is sufficient in Jesus Christ. Amen.

God's Man in Action: Before eating, simply say the word *grace*. Reflect on its truth, power, and sufficiency.

An Appointment
with Disappointment

Romans 7:15–25

We just passed a sign that welcomed us to the state of Pennsylvania. My wife, Chiara, announced to the backseat filled with three anxious children that we had arrived at our vacation destination. After a couple of cheers, Benjamin was quiet. He looked out the window a while, scratched his head, and then with disappointment said, "I thought everything would look like pencils in 'Pencil-vania.' "

While he was disappointed, I was fascinated with his observation about "Pencil-vania." His expectations weren't met. As we planned that particular vacation, he must have had some very interesting concepts in his mind when we spoke of our destination. He had a right to be disappointed. Although I had never made that particular observation, I have been disappointed a time or two over another state ... the state of my life as a Christian man and father. Although pencils may not be a part of Pennsylvania, there is no doubt that Christ is a part of a *Christ*ian.

*Christ*ians are to pattern their love after Christ's

perfect love. *Christ*ians have put off the things that are of this world. *Christ*ians forgive as Christ forgives. The *Christ*ian's life is one of heartfelt worship. The call to be a *Christ*ian is a full-time commitment. How often I disappoint myself and God through my sin as a *Christ*ian man and father.

The apostle Paul describes the daily struggle so well when he writes:

> I do not understand what I do. For what I want to do I do not do, but what I hate I do. ... I have the desire to do what is good, but I cannot carry it out. For what I do is not the good I want to do; no, the evil I do not want to do— this I keep on doing. ... What a wretched man I am! Who will rescue me from this body of death? Thanks be to God—through Jesus Christ our Lord! (Romans 7:15, 18–19, 24–25)

Sounds like a child's game of tug-of-war between our old sinful nature and the new creation we have become as God's children marked with His perfect name. If we only look at ourselves, we will have a constant appointment with disappointment. We are sinners who have failed Christ, His name, and His calling.

Instead of expecting disappointment in our lives, we need to take our eyes off ourselves and look to Christ. Standing in His presence and perfection, we need to confess our failings and turn to Him for forgiveness and grace. In Christ's presence we find the way to live a Christ-like life. We find His much needed forgiveness and the power to forgive others. In Christ we find a love and a life that is a pattern for our living and loving. There we find Christ covering our imperfections with His perfection and righteousness. When looking to Christ, we will not be disappointed.

I feel bad that Benjamin was disappointed on our vacation. I also feel bad as I call myself a *Christ*ian but am not always Christ-like. But that is also when I feel a call to repentance as the Lord leads me to make a right turn and welcomes me with open arms to a new state where I see Christ is all and is in all ... myself included. What a great state in which to make our home. We won't be disappointed.

Father to Father: Father, You have placed Your Son's name on me. I am not deserving of a holy name, but I wear it with boldness in the state of grace in which I live. Amen.

God's Man in Action: Consider ordering a personalized license plate for your vehicle that witnesses the state of grace in which you live. Some suggestions: 4GIVEN, ESD14U, GRACE, ATPEAS, etc. At least have fun thinking of the possibilities.

Chapter and Verse

Acts 20:32

Parents experience a variety of new chapters in their lives and in the lives of their children. Milestones mark accomplishments and create memories for the scrapbook on the shelf and the one in the heart. These emotional and exciting times give us reason to celebrate God's goodness. These new chapters also mean changes that will affect each of us.

After the whirlwind events surrounding the birth of her son, Mary "treasured up all these things and pondered them in her heart" (Luke 2:19). That wasn't the only time she would do this. Remember the trip Mary, Joseph, and Jesus took to Jerusalem for the Lord's Passover when Jesus was 12 years old? (See Luke 2:41–52.) After the Passover, Jesus stayed in town to sit with the teachers in the temple courts. When they found Him, Mary asked, "Son, why have You treated us like this? Your father and I have been anxiously searching for You" (v. 48).

Jesus responded, "Why were you searching for Me? … Didn't you know I had to be in My Father's house?" (v. 49). His parents didn't fully understand what He was saying, but once again, Mary treasured all these things in her heart. It was a chapter in His life. He was moving from boy to man, from a carpenter who hammered nails into wood to a Savior who died nailed to wood.

Mary and Joseph must have given Jesus wonderful, Spirit-directed gifts to celebrate these chapters in His life. This particular chapter ends by noting that Jesus grew in wisdom and stature and in favor with God and men.

Consider some of the chapters in the lives of your children. How did or will the chapter affect you?

- Birth
- Baptism
- First steps
- First day at day care, preschool, or kinder-garten
- First public performance (musical, art, sports, speech, etc.)
- Confirmation
- First date
- Graduation (kindergarten, junior high, high school, college)
- Marriage
- Birth of grandchildren

Since new chapters in our children's lives are reasons to celebrate, gift-giving is appropriate. A free gift that keeps on giving is found in Acts 20:32. Paul is moving away from a church he "birthed" through God's power. It was a new chapter for Paul and the young church in Ephesus. As they moved together into this new chapter, he left them this gift: "Now I commit you to God and to the word of His grace, which can build you up and give you an inheritance among all those who are sanctified." After giving them a gift by committing them to God's grace, Paul prayed with them. They shared tears and hugs. Then his church family accompanied him to the ship to embark on a new chapter in his life. With that kind of send off, I'm confident that, like Jesus, they grew in wisdom and stature and in favor with God and men.

Committing our loved ones to God and walking with them into a new chapter of life—what a wonderful gift to give to celebrate God moving us into every new chapter of our lives.

Father to Father: Father God, thanks for reasons to celebrate Your goodness in our lives. Lead us into new chapters of life as we commit our lives and families to Your gracious will. In Jesus' name. Amen.

God's Man in Action: As you celebrate each chapter of life, wrap and give a gift that contains the words, "Congratulations and God's blessings! My gift for you is found in Acts 20:32."

The Trip to the Big City

John 14:1–3

T he voice on the phone invited us to a family wedding in New York City. Instantly, the ol' stomach butterflies were awakened.

New York City. *The* city. The Big Apple. The city that doesn't sleep.

I had never been to *the* city. Apples aren't my favorite fruit. And I need my sleep.

Cities do not make me nervous, but New York City gave me the jitters. With the help of news reports, movies, watching Mets games on cable, and a vivid imagination, I had drawn a mental picture of what *the* city was all about.

I had a month until the plane touched down at LaGuardia. That was plenty of time for my mind to walk through every possible way to get mugged. I checked prices for mace, money belts, and bodyguards. I practiced screaming until I was hoarse. Despite my preparations, I was nervous as we boarded the plane.

From the time we landed until we got to the hotel, I checked my Captain Marvel secret hide-a-way, bullet-proof wallet 327 times. It was unharmed, still strapped to my chest (although the reinforced, three-inch chain and lock that held it in place were quite uncomfortable).

The next morning, as my father-in-law and I walked down the street, I observed everything that moved. What was that knocking sound? It was coming from inside the trunk of the car parked next to me. I couldn't believe it. As the knocking continued, I pictured the poor soul inside, badly beaten, bound, and gagged. We couldn't just ignore his cries and walk on by. We knocked on the trunk. "Are you okay? Can you hear us?" No response. We knocked again. He knocked again. "Are you okay?" My father-in-law put his ear to the trunk. We held our breath ... until we started laughing. Out from under the car came a man with a hammer. He was fixing his muffler.

The rest of the trip was great. The wedding was beautiful. I traded my New York-proof wallet for an "I love NY" bumper sticker. Although I had spent so much time fretting over the trip, it turned out to be thoroughly enjoyable. In fact, I couldn't wait to return.

It wasn't the first time I had gotten worked up about a trip. When I was a child, I used to get worked up when a voice from the pulpit would tell me that we were going to the New Jerusalem for a wedding. Instantly, the stomach butterflies joined me in the pew and they wouldn't let up all day. Something about eternity frightened me. Maybe it was death, I don't know. Heaven was okay, but the sermons and the thought of "forever" bothered me. No one knew my secret fear.

Today I can't wait for heaven. One of my favorite prayers is simply, "Come, Lord Jesus ... *quickly!*" What comfort it is to know that I am in eternal life right now because of my Spirit-created faith in heaven's host, Jesus Christ.

I wish I would have made someone aware of my childhood concerns and questions. It would have saved me from nightmares of giant heavenly cows and bee stings (the land flowing with milk and honey). Fire and brimstone preachers, St. Peter-at-the-gate jokes, images from Revelation, and a vivid imagination can lead children (and fathers) to some odd conclusions. Through prayer, discussion, and Bible study we can look forward to the trip and to the perfect destination. It begins by experiencing a portion of God's heaven on earth through His promises, peace, and life. By living daily in God's perfect love and talking openly with one another and with heaven's Architect, we can rest in peace tonight and eternally. For heaven's sake, and ours, let's be prepared for the joyful journey that leads us home.

Father to Father: Father, Your presence brings a bit of heaven into my daily life. Thanks. Help me lead my family joyfully in the trip that brings us *home* through our guide, Jesus. Amen.

God's Man in Action: Lead a family discussion about heaven. God's Spirit will guide you.

A Pfamily Psalm

Psalm 136

Psalm 136 is a prayer of praise to God. It's a celebration of God's forever love. It's a reminder of God's grace. It's thanksgiving inspired. It's a word of encouragement for the future. It's a psalm of repetition—26 times the phrase "His love endures forever" is proclaimed. The psalmist gives thanks to the Lord and reviews His mighty acts from creation to the Promised Land. It's a psalm for the family of God, about God and His family. So is this.

Give thanks to the Lord, for He is good.
His love endures forever.

Give thanks to the Lord of our family.
His love endures forever.

Thank Him who knew us before we were a family:
His love endures forever.

Who breathed into us the breath of life,
Filling our lungs with air
And our hearts with an eternal hope.
His love endures forever.

Give thanks to Him who allowed our children
To take first steps and us, by His Spirit,
To follow in His steps;
His love endures forever.

Who created the unseen sign of the cross
  That marks us as ones redeemed
  By Christ the crucified;
  His love endures forever.

Who gives us shelter and food while covering us
With His love as we drink from His living water;
  His love endures forever.

Who carried us through thousands of diapers
  And hundreds of childhood stages,
Through first words, school tests, lost teeth,
  And lasting memories.
  His love endures forever.

Thank Him who carried us
  through weeks of chicken pox
And heals all our diseases;
  His love endures forever.

Who compassionately leads us
  Through times of darkness and family deaths
Directly into the eternal promise of life;
  His love endures forever.

Who graciously entrusts us
  with more than we need
And more than we ask for;
  His love endures forever.

Thank Him who gives us reason to focus
On what lies ahead
  His love endures forever.

Walking together, hand and heart in His,
Knowing there is forgiveness
  For patience lost and guilt found,

Along with a myriad of other sins—
Some of which we know and
   some known only to Him.
      His love endures forever.

We walk with confidence and joy
As a family within His family.
      His love endures forever.

To Him who gave His life for this and all families
Be all praise, honor, and thanksgiving for
      His love endures forever.

Give thanks to the Lord, for He is good!
      His love endures forever.

Father to Father: Pray the psalm with your family.

God's Man in Action: Write "His love endures forever" on a piece of paper and keep it where you need it most. Also write your own pfamily or pfather's psalm.

ABCs for Dads

Revelation 22:13

Jesus referred to the first and last letter of the Greek alphabet when describing who He is and what He is about. He is the First and the Last, the Alpha and the Omega, and everything in between. We should strive to be all that He would want us to be as fathers. With that in mind, here are some ABCs for dads.

Accept your children as they are, which will encourage them to be all the Lord wants them to be.

Bible-base your parenting, marriage, job, relationships, thoughts, and daily life.

Compassion is not a sign of weakness but one of great strength in the Lord, whose heart goes out to you.

Discipline in love. It is a necessary tool for a father who loves his children.

Example. Your actions and words have a powerful, lasting effect on your children. Pattern your life after the Lord's since your children follow the pattern you leave them.

Forgiven and forgiving is your heritage through Christ's gifts. Share the gifts.

God-fearing. Stand in awe of the ultimate Father as you father.

Hope in the certainty of God's promises as you walk daily as a parent and as His dearly loved child.

Interest in your children's interests says to them, "I love you!"

Joke around more. Lighten up!

Know your family—their needs, wants, joys, fears, likes, and dislikes.

Love. Nothing more needs to be said.

Mom-lover. Love your children's mother.

No. It's a necessary word at times, but not at all times.

Oasis. Create a godly home for your children that is an oasis in the midst of their wilderness days.

Play!

Quake in God's presence. You are on holy ground.

Rejoice! I will say it again, *rejoice!*

Servant father. You are called to a position of authority. You also were called to serve.

Thankful. Oh, give thanks, father, for the showers of God's blessings.

Undermine the plans that Satan has to undermine your family.

Verify the love you have for your family. Do it daily in words and actions.

Worship the Lord faithfully and joyfully with your family.

X. Sometimes there are no words to describe the calling to be a godly father.

Yearn to follow closer in your Savior's footsteps.

Zest. Add this to your personal prayer list and to your life.

Father to Father: Through Your Son, O God, You are the Alpha and Omega and everything in between. May Your Holy Spirit work in me to help me be all that You want me to be. I love everything about You, Lord, from A to Z. Amen.

God's Man in Action: Make up your own family A-to-Z list. Keep it visible in your home to remind family members of your goals and calling.

How Far among So Many?

John 6:1–13

He always knew the answer to the question before he read it. Amazing. He held an envelope up and said something like, "The answer is: 'A parakeet with laryngitis and sending a child to college.' " Then he opened the envelope and read the question "What are two things that don't go cheep (cheap)?" Carnack the Magnificent. Amazing.

Okay, not so amazing. He used cue cards.

There was another one with a similar ability. He didn't use cue cards, but He took His cue from His Father. He knew the answer to the questions before the questions were asked.

He tried it with Philip, when more than 5,000 people gathered around him. He gave Philip's faith a test and said, "The answer is, 'Trust Me.' " Then He asked, "Where shall we buy bread for these people to eat?" (He already knew the answer.) Philip looked for an answer. He checked his wallet and searched his brain. He scrounged for answers while Andrew brought a portion of the recipe for serving this multitude: One small boy, five small barley loaves, and two small fish. He brought those items to the main ingredient—one large-hearted miracle worker.

Now it was Andrew's turn to ask the question but, not so amazingly, he didn't know the answer before he asked it: "How far will they go among so many?"

Today we gather around the Lord with the multitudes. We come as people who are easily overwhelmed by the events around us.

So much stress ... so little relief. So many voices demanding my time ... so little time.

So many anxieties ... so few peace givers. So many diapers ... such a little child.

So many bills ... such a small paycheck. So many sins ... so few forgivers.

So many dying of hunger ... so few that are willing to feed them.

So few. So small. So insignificant. How far will it go among so many?

Overwhelmed, we often miss the one who has the answer. We miss the yeastlike main ingredient that can feed the multitudes. How often we miss the miracles of the one

- who provides living water that eternally quenches the thirst of the multitudes.

- who brings together one man and one woman and creates a Christian family.

- who takes 66 books and one Spirit and feeds the spiritually hungry, empowers the weak, and answers the questions.

- who took six days, created a world, and added an entire day for physical and spiritual rest.

- who takes one small piece of unleavened bread, one taste of wine, and one sacrificial death and feeds the guilt-ridden multitude of souls with forgiveness and strength for their faith.
- who takes three nails and one death by crucifixion and gives life to the multitudes.

How far will one Savior go among so many? The answer comes from the one who knows the answers to all our questions. He bids us to place them all into His hands so He may bless them and feed us with all the answers we need.

We have a Savior who went so far as to enter gracefully from the glories of heaven to a hellish world ... to a death bed of nails and a tomb in rocks ... to the depths of hell and the heights of heaven ... to the very end of the age ... and beyond. That's how far one Savior went for so many. Amazing, isn't He? He will stop at nothing to feed the multitude in your house or His world. He hopes you will stop at nothing in working toward that same goal.

Father to Father: Feed me by Your grace. By Your Spirit's guidance, use me to feed my family and the multitudes. In the strong name of Jesus. Amen.

God's Man in Action: As you make those "stop on the way home for bread" trips, remember the price of the bread and drop 10 percent (or 10 pennies) in a coffee can. After a year, give the money to a food pantry or a hot-meal program.

Watch Where You Camp

Exodus 16:1–5

I have to admit that when my son opted not to participate in Scouting, I wasn't disappointed. It has nothing to do with Boy Scouts in general. I just knew that someday we'd have to go on a father-son camping trip (probably two or three).

I've been camping, and I've also heard plenty of camping stories. This results in a couple of theories about camping. One is that if you want it to rain, snow, or turn cold, go camping. The other theory is that camping leads to lying. Campers spend weekends fighting storms, floods, gale force winds, or record-breaking temperatures, and they return to tell everyone about the fun they had. Who am I to judge the truthfulness of their statements?

From my few camping experiences, I have learned one lesson: You need to watch where you camp. Picking a campsite is an art. I've witnessed campers checking the ground for hardness and slope. They measure wind velocity before setting up. They measure the distance from the campsite to the water source, the campfire, the nearest wild animal residence, and natural rest room sites. These factors are all well and good.

When God was leading His people through the wilderness toward the Promised Land, they did a lot of camping. There is one campsite that is particularly interesting. Exodus 16 tells us that the whole Israelite community set out from Elim and came to the Desert of Sin. What a location to camp—Sin! I'm sure the Israelite comedians had a field day with that one. "Hi! Do you live in Sin?" If I had been Moses' travel agent, I think I would have advised him to watch where he camps and avoid Sin. That is good advice for all of us traveling to the Promised Land.

Our heavenly Travel Agent has warned us to watch where we camp. Satan sets up alluring sites as we travel, hoping that we will choose his location. Satan knows our weak points and what will attract us to his desert of sin. The apostle Paul reminds us, "Do not give the devil a foothold" (Ephesians 4:27).

"Don't play with fire" is also good camping advice. If Satan has found a weak spot in your life in regard to alcohol, don't plan a business lunch at a bar. If you are tempted to sleep in on Sunday morning, don't camp out so late on Saturday night. If you are dealing with overeating, avoid certain aisles at the grocery store. If you easily fall into the sin of gossip, don't camp out where it flows freely during your work breaks. If you struggle with patience at home, try to plan family activities that aren't so stressful. If you have problems with pornography, find a gas station where you pay at the pump to avoid the tempting magazines behind the counter.

Watch where you camp—pass by the Desert of Sin and head to the Oasis of Forgiveness. Do not give the devil a foothold. Do give your life—thoughts, words, and actions—to Jesus Christ. Ask Him to serve as your travel agent and companion as He leads you past the deserts of sin to the Promised Land.

Father to Father: I need help choosing the places where my family and I camp. Grant me wisdom, guidance, and strength as we travel together to Your Promised Land. In Jesus' name. Amen.

God's Man in Action: Pick an upcoming weekend and make plans to camp out with your children—on their bedroom floor, in the backyard, or possibly at a real campsite. (Warning: Bring warm rain gear.)

Father of the Bride

Ephesians 5:25–32

As a pastor, I have the best view in the house (of God) when the bride comes down the aisle. There are no relatives with big hats blocking my view. My perspective is straight on, not from an awkward angle. As all eyes are trying to get a glimpse of the beautiful bride, her dress, and bouquet, I watch Dad coming down that aisle. I have my reasons.

The church I serve has a long aisle that brides love. It gives me plenty of time to imagine myself in the father's place with my daughter on my arm. What goes through the mind of a father walking his daughter down the aisle? If, God-willing, I have that opportunity, I wonder where my thoughts will be. I know that tears will probably be in my eyes.

I don't mind sharing that I cried my eyes out at the Steve Martin remake of "Father of the Bride." I kept picturing myself as the father with my daughter, Sarah, getting married. The most touching part was the family dinner. As the daughter was talking, her father kept seeing her as his little girl in pigtails. Now, when Sarah wears pigtails, my thoughts turn to my possible future role as father of the bride.

As I watch a father escort his daughter down the aisle, I wonder if he's recalling the days when she was a little girl in pigtails or the days he cheered her team to victory or the days he dried her tears after a fall. Maybe he's thinking about how to handle the fact that his daughter is going home with that man at the end of the aisle. With all the fancy clothes and decorations, I guess some dads also have wedding bills dancing in their heads.

I enjoyed reading a business-style card that a local caterer supplied to the father of one bride. It read: "I am the father of the bride. Nobody's paying much attention to me today, but I can assure you that I am getting my share of attention, for the banks and several business firms are watching me very closely."

The father of the bride usually isn't the center of attention. Sometimes that's the case with another Father of the bride. In the Bible, Jesus often is referred to as the Bridegroom and the church as His bride. People may pay a lot of attention to the important role of the church in this world, and rightly so. Much ink has been spilled on the topic of Christ's bride. Wars have been started over her. People have been persecuted for this bride.

The problem comes when we put so much emphasis on the church/bride that we forget about the Bridegroom, without whom there would be no bride. We forget about the Father of the bride, who sacrificed—at great cost—His only Son so the bride could have life eternally. We forget that the bride, Christ's church, must keep her eyes on Jesus Christ and His Father who sent Him. In the case of this divine wedding, when Christ comes to claim His bride, the entire world will be in attendance. And no one will be able to take their eyes off the wedding party—bride, Bridegroom, or Father of the bride.

(Sniff. Sniff.) Excuse me. Sarah just walked in, and she has her hair in pigtails.

Father to Father: Dear Father of the bride, I look forward to the wedding feast when Christ returns to claim His bride, the church. Until that day, grant Your Spirit's guidance to keep my eyes focused on You as I join You in making daily preparations for the big event. In the Bridegroom's name. Amen.

God's Man in Action: Look at your wedding photographs and note your father-in-law. What do you think he's thinking? Don't forget to notice how beautiful your wife looked—and share that thought with her.

The Sound of Weeping, Crying, and Mashing of Potatoes

Ezra 3:10–13

E very once in a while, as I step onto the front porch at the end of the day, I know what to anticipate. That's because I can hear what's going on behind the closed door. While it's difficult to distinguish if it's a joyful noise or sounds of displeasure, it is noisy.

With trepidation I turn the doorknob. As the door opens, the noise grows louder. No one notices that I'm home. I survey the situation. No wonder I couldn't decipher the type of noise. One child is in time out, weeping dramatically with head buried in small arms. Another shouts with joy after dunking a mini-basketball a record 52 times. The third child's noise seems to be a mixture of singing, shouting, and laughing combined with television noise and the loud hum of the electric beater mashing potatoes (with my wife's assistance). Ah, all is well on the home front.

Ezra was part of a similar home-front experience. He and many of God's exiled people were returning to their homeland, Israel. Ezra was part of the team supervising the rebuilding of God's temple in Jerusalem. Ezra 3:11–13 describes the completing of the temple's foundation:

> With praise and thanksgiving they sang to the LORD: "He is good; His love to Israel endures forever." And all the people gave a great shout of praise to the LORD, because the foundation of the house of the LORD was laid. But many of the older priests and Levites and family heads, who had seen the former temple, wept aloud when they saw the foundation of this temple being laid, while many others shouted for joy. No one could distinguish the sound of the shouts of joy from the sound of weeping, because the people made so much noise. And the sound was heard far away.

Usually, I don't do well with a lot of noise. It can signify that things are out of control. In the situation I described earlier, my wife had everything under control. She knew where everyone was and what was happening. Children were being children. They were having fun, singing, and being disciplined. Walking in from the outside made it appear out of control.

For Ezra and the other Israelites, things could appear to be out of control. Yet God had everything under control. Even while the Israelites were in exile,

God was in control. He is still in control—so in control that He hears every tear that falls to the ground and every joyful belly laugh. He knows every heart and its motive. He is in control.

God knew my feelings and how the events of my day would affect my response as I walked into the house. He knew that some of the tears of the Israelites were tears of joy and praise for His goodness. He also knew which tears were of sadness for the tragic events of the past that were remembered that day. He knew if my son, who had misbehaved, was truly sorry for his sin. He rejoiced in the energy of my daughter. He was in control of the body of my basketball-shooting son, for He had created it. And He was in control of supper, working through my wife and the food He had provided. He was in control.

In the midst of situations, events, and noisy days that seem to be out of control, it is a most comforting truth to rest in: God is in control.

Father to Father: Father, Your knowledge is too lofty for me to attain. I praise You for that. Take control of what I want to control. I trust and pray in Jesus' name. Amen.

God's Man in Action: In a creative and loud way, join your family in making a joyful noise to the Lord today.

Sing a Song

Colossians 3:15–18

In this age most families would get a chuckle out of seeing the Walton family sitting around the piano singing after actually eating together.

We seem quite a distance from that picture. I hope that families haven't completely lost the fine art of singing together. The apostle Paul encourages us to teach each other with wisdom as we "sing psalms, hymns and spiritual songs with gratitude in [our] hearts to God" (Colossians 3:16).

I realize that some individuals and families aren't musical (unless they're alone in the car with the windows rolled up). Our family enjoys making a joyful noise to the Lord, windows rolled up or not.

I thought it would be fun to take the tune of a vacation Bible school song, "You Are by My Side," and write a family song. If you or your family enjoys singing, I encourage you to try the same. When you're done, get in the car, roll *down* the windows, and make a joyful noise to the Lord.

Tim Wesemann

Karen Marie

1. Ho - ly Fa - ther, You have made us one,
2. O dear Fa - ther, guard our house to - day.
3. Je - sus, Sav - ior, on the cross You died.
4. Liv - ing Je - sus, East - er morn You rose,
5. Ho - ly Spir - it, wis - dom we do seek.
6. Hear us, Spir - it, joy - ful - ly we sing.

As a fam - 'ly liv - ing in Your Son.
Watch our fam - 'ly— all we do and say.
In Your blood - bought sac - ri - fice we hide.
Claim - ing vic - t'ry o - ver all our woes.
Fore - casts some - times look so ver - y bleak.
To You, bold - ly, gifts of praise we bring,

Cause our faith to grow in what You have done.
Lead us faith - ful - ly as we walk Your way.
You for - give our sins; draw us to Your side.
Sin and death You beat and our dev - 'lish foes.
You're our source of strength through - out ev - 'ry week.
As you car - ry us, as on ea - gles' wings.

Ho - ly Fa - ther, You have made us one.
O dear Fa - ther, guard our house to - day.
Je - sus, Sav - ior, on the cross You died.
Liv - ing Je - sus, East - er morn You rose.
Ho - ly Spir - it, wis - dom we do seek.
Hear us, Spir - it, joy - ful - ly we sing.

Father to Father: Father, no matter our pitch or talent, may the lives of my family be a beautiful song of praise to You. Amen.

God's Man in Action: Remember that grumpiness and singing don't easily mix. The next time the grumpies invite them- selves to your house, chase them away by making a joyful noise to the Lord—on key or off.

157

Joseph's Prayer as a Stepfather

Matthew 1:18–25

Dear Father in heaven,

Blessed are You, Lord of the universe. My soul praises Your holy name. I offer this prayer to You as one who feels very blessed, yet very confused. Is this all a dream? My Mary—pregnant? The Messiah whom we have longed for is living within her?

There is so much I have to say. There is so much I don't understand. I need Your help, Father. The child is Yours, yet You have entrusted Him to my care. So much is going through my mind.

His mother and I will have little time to grow as husband and wife before this child is born. I struggle with that, Lord. Children take so much time and attention. Will my wife and I be able to handle the stresses of marriage and parenthood at the same time? I guess with that question I am really asking You for help.

As You know, our families aren't exactly thrilled about this arrangement. Help them, Lord, to be supportive. We need their wisdom, love, and guidance.

With a child comes an additional financial burden. I

pray for my business, Lord. I place its future into Your hands. Allow me to be a good provider for my family.

And what about this child's future? Should I teach Him my carpentry skills? Later in life will it make a difference that He knows the feel of wood and nails? You are full of wonderful surprises, and I hope that as a stepfather, I will pass that gift on to my family.

This one born of Mary will be the Son of Man yet the very Son of God. So many prayers I have offered to You for the Messiah, and all the while You were molding me to be His stepfather. Use my upbringing and past experiences to prepare me for this high calling. I offer You my eternal praise.

I do not have all the answers, but I know that You do. And that is enough for me. I am uncertain why You have called me to this role, but I am certain that You will lead me in the ways that I should go. I realize that the road will not always be easy, but it will be hard to miss Your plan if I focus on the road map of Your Word. What wonderful gifts You have entrusted to my care!

This calling is from You. I am so undeserving. With great humility I accept what You have revealed to me in this high calling. I go forward, step by step, trusting in Your guidance.

You have a wonderful way for this stepfather and all stepfathers to view their calling. The child in my home is Yours, entrusted to my care. I am called to be a godly example. While I step into this role, lead me to keep this household in step with Your holy will and ways. As

I respect who He is, I am respecting You. As I honor You, I am teaching Him to honor You.

Lead me, Father, in Your ways. Great is Your faithfulness. I go forward, trusting in Your lead, step by precious step. Amen.

Father to Father: Father, be with all Your children who are stepparents. Support them and their families with Your heaven-sent words of help, hope, and happiness. Amen.

God's Man in Action: Contact someone who has been blessed with the role of stepfather. Encourage him in his calling. Step into the role of Christian friend to him through your contact and prayers.

Loneliness

Joshua 1:9

*L*oneliness is a lonely word. It even sounds lonely when you say it. Stuck inside that word are three other "lonely" words: *lone ... one ...* and *I*. Everyone is vulnerable to loneliness. Our thoughts might turn immediately to widows and widowers, singles, or those who are divorced. But they aren't the only ones who face loneliness.

Sometimes the most lonely person we know may be surrounded by people. Sometimes the more crowded our lives are the lonelier we become.

Unfortunately, people rarely share with others that they are feeling lonely so we may be unaware of another's pain. Sharing those thoughts and feelings (not in a complaining way, but sincerely) is a big step in dealing with loneliness.

Fathers aren't exempt from loneliness. A man can be surrounded by family, co-workers, and friends and yet still feel lonely. To make matters worse, fathers typically would be the least likely to share with someone that they struggle with loneliness.

Loneliness also can be a heavenly nudge that pushes us back to the one who promised never to leave or forsake us. God can use bouts of loneliness to encourage us to lean on His presence even more. Loneliness tempts us to focus on ourselves so that we don't recognize and acknowledge God's presence in our lives. Loneliness also causes us to become so drawn into ourselves that we forget we are part of the body of Christ. We are surrounded by people who care and want to help in the best way possible.

It is extremely important to fight the temptation to focus only on ourselves. When we bite at that temptation, we must realize that we aren't alone. We have chosen Satan's presence over God's.

On the other hand, God has given us the ability, desire, and joy to break down the barriers of loneliness in someone else's life. We need to be aware of the needs of those battling loneliness while listening for their disguised cries. Pray that they would see the need to share their feelings with you or another Christian friend.

Another of Satan's temptations for those battling loneliness is the quick fix, which is often an ungodly solution. Satan loves to strike when we are down.

Christian author Tim Hansel says, "Loneliness does not always come from emptiness. Sometimes it is because we are too full ... full of ourselves. Full of activity ... full of distractions. Paradoxically, if I want to heal the loneliness in my life, I've got to get away ... to be alone with God."

What a marvelous God we have! Being *alone* with

Him is one of His cures for loneliness. When you travel through that barren land of loneliness, remember there is help. Your ever-present companion shares His promises and presence with you. Seek Him out. Seek out ways to help others who are lonely. When Jesus walked this earth, He experienced many lonely feelings and events. Your compassionate friend can truly relate to your feelings and has the means to help.

Yes, the word *loneliness* sounds lonely. But on the other hand, how sweet the name of Jesus sounds!

Father to Father: Father, I feel lonely when (complete the sentence). At those times, may Your Spirit guide me to Your Word, which tells me (complete the sentence). Thank You for Your presence and Your promise to never leave me or forsake me. I love You. Amen.

God's Man in Action: Write a note to someone who may be struggling with loneliness. "Thinking of you and lifting you up in prayer" would be a simple message to include.

Bugs!

Ephesians 5:8–11

The screen door is a favorite hangout for the neighborhood June bugs (not their technical name). They hang there, attracted to the kitchen light until they fall. They often land on their backs, flailing their little legs. If you are familiar with these bugs, you know they can be very annoying.

When things "bug" us, it's easy to hang aimlessly until we fall. There we lay, flailing around in a "bugged" state.

The following is a list of noninsect "bugs" that often hang around fathers. They are attracted to artificial light. To destroy them, expose them to the true Light of the world. There is hope for whatever is bugging you with the "true light" of God's Word.

Technical name: *Runinonemptee* (stress bug)

Usual hangouts: Work, rush-hour traffic, deadlines, overextended schedules, parents, etc.

True-Light bug destroyer: Matthew 11:28; Isaiah 40:28–31; Psalm 23

Technical name: *Pacesdaflor* (worry bug)

Usual hangouts: Home, work, minds, parents of teens, teens with parents, nervous people, upset stomachs, doctors' offices, etc.

True-Light bug destroyer: Matthew 6:25–34; Proverbs 3:5

Technical name: *Iamnil* (poor-image bug)

Usual hangouts: Minds, dominant personalities, unloving situations, trips to the past, etc.

True-Light bug destroyer: 2 Corinthians 5:17; Ephesians 4:20–24; Psalm 40:1–2

Technical name: *Outafundz* (financial bug)

Usual hangouts: Unemployed, retired, families with children in college, April 15, bill drawer, etc.

True-Light bug destroyer: Philippians 4:19; Psalm 69:33; Matthew 6:8, 25–34

Technical name: *Alwayzangree* (bitterness bug)

Usual hangouts: Unforgiving hearts, enemies, hurting families, open wounds from past, unloving hearts, etc.

True-Light bug destroyer: Colossians 3:13; Ephesians 4:31; Matthew 6:14–15

Technical name: *Myphault* (guilt bug)

Usual hangouts: Minds, past sins, guilt trips, memories, arguments when past is brought up, etc.

True-Light bug destroyer: Romans 8:1; Isaiah 43:25; Psalm 103:12

These are a few "bugs" you might find hanging around your life. Stop flailing and take hold of the Light found in God's Word. Rejoice in God's peace that helps cure all that bugs you.

Father to Father: At this moment, Father, there are so many things that are bothering me or have the potential to do so. I will name them now, giving them to You ... Amen.

God's Man in Action: On small pieces of paper write items that are bugging family members. Tape them around your house. Pray about them. When your prayers have been answered, remove the paper. Keep the "destroyed bugs" in a jar to remind you of God's power.

Heavenly Medicine

Zephaniah 3:17

Your wife called. She took your child to the hospital." "The boss wants to see you." "I need your decision now." "The doctor said I've had a miscarriage." "Your parents really need to be in a nursing home." "The school principal would like to meet with you." "The funeral service is about to begin." "I'm tired of all the arguing!"

Just reading these statements could cause a major case of anxiety. You may have heard similar words and can easily relate to the feelings that accompany them. Such statements often are accompanied by skyrocketing blood pressure, emotions that work overtime, and frayed nerves. What a great time for a dose of medicine—a dose of heavenly medicine that can't be found in a medicine cabinet.

The Old Testament prophet Zephaniah reminds us of news that is easy to swallow and has life-changing results: "The LORD your God is with you, He is mighty to save. He will take great delight in you, He will quiet you with His love, He will rejoice over you with singing" (Zephaniah 3:17).

We often prescribe similar medicine to our children.

Consider their reaction and your prescription for healing when they trip on the cement, when they have to get a shot at the doctor's, when they're sure there is a monster under the bed, when bullies attack, or when the chicken pox pop out. Holding them tightly, you say, "Daddy is here. I'll save you from that mean old monster. I love you. It will be okay. *(wipe tear)* I'm here. Calm down. *(singing)* You are my sunshine, my only sunshine. You make me happy when skies are gray. You'll never know, dear, how much I love you. Please don't take my sunshine away."

God the Father has raised His share of children (in more ways than one). His words and actions are there no matter what His children's ages. He is the same loving, protecting, saving Father to infants as well as to fathers. His heavenly medicine comes in an extra-strength prescription.

God will not only be there for us, He can save us. He can relate to the stresses we face because He faced them on earth. As God, He can save us from them or preserve us throughout the trial. He delights in His children. As we sing His praises, He is rejoicing over us with singing. What a great mental picture!

As God holds us in His arms, we feel safe and protected. We feel hope in His powerful presence. And He quiets us down. He calms our frayed nerves and lowers the blood pressure. His unconditional, medicinal love brings us peace amidst Satan and the world trying to make us go to war.

The presence, power, and promises of our Lord bring newfound help in the most difficult situations. God is present. He is in control. He will go to battle for us and with us. He has saving power. He offers a peace that we can find nowhere else. Confidently, we rest in His arms, in His loving faithfulness, while He miraculously quiets us with His love. And while He holds us, He is rejoicing over us with singing.

Father to Father: Father, I have and will spend a lot of time striving to comfort and quiet my children. Remind me that You are there with the same heavenly medicine to calm my troubled days and nights. Quiet me, Lord. Come near me and save me from my enemies. Heal me. I need You to hold me. Let me hear Your singing, for I am hurting now. Amen.

God's Man in Action: Find an old medicine bottle and on the label write, "Zephaniah 3:17." Keep it near you as a reminder of God's prescription of heavenly medicine.

Water Works

Acts 2:38–39

For three summers I guided white-water canoe trips in the mountains of North Carolina. Our crew knew we could have an interesting time when a father and son shared a canoe. Often—not always—fathers and sons had a hard time working together. When problems occurred, it seemed to stem from both men wanting to be in control. We witnessed several arguments from canoes manned by strong-willed males who seemed to know it all.

I recall a unique incident that happened on a rapids affectionately named "Captain Crunch." It was a great setting with trees hanging over the river and a huge rock (Captain Crunch) at the end of the run. If you didn't catch the eddy, the canoe would have a rude meeting with the Captain! As guides, we would station ourselves on the rocks with safety ropes to assist any canoes that capsized.

As this particular father-son canoe headed for the white water, the occupants were complaining and yelling at each other. In the midst of it all, they capsized the canoe right at the top of the rapid. They panicked as the white water carried them on their backs toward Captain Crunch. Arms flailing, they tried to grab a branch or our safety ropes. Finally, the father's right hand grabbed something—it was his left arm. Flailing around, looking to be saved, he had caught his own arm.

As a guide I had seen people grab canoes, ropes, branches, and people for safety, but this was a first. It wasn't the first time I had witnessed someone trying to save himself. More men than women seem to be in this boat.

When it comes to saving, we need to learn that the manly answer for us, or our families, is not, "Be a man—pull yourself up by your own bootstraps." The manly answer when it comes to salvation is a godly answer. We are saved by grace, through faith, not by our own works (Ephesians 2:8–9). No matter how strong or in control we are, we can't save ourselves. No, the only way to salvation is by holding on for dear life to our Savior, Jesus Christ. That power comes from God's Spirit, not us.

It reminds me of the story of Peter walking on the water (Matthew 14:25–33). When Peter took his eyes off Jesus, he began to sink and cried, "Lord, save me!" Jesus reached out and caught Peter. In this water he was completely helpless until saved by the out-stretched hand of Jesus.

God does His saving in water. God's Word, His Spirit, and the waters of Baptism work to save us from our sins and ourselves. We are saved by a Spirit-created faith that trusts totally in Jesus, who stretched out His arms on the cross and saved us.

If you're out of control or fighting for control, drop everything and take hold of the outstretched hand of your Savior. He will save you and gracefully lead you through the life-giving water.

Father to Father: Send Your Spirit so I can hold on for dear life to my Savior. I trustingly place all I am and have into His outstretched hands of salvation. Amen.

God's Man in Action: Wash the dishes tonight. Watch them sink into the water. As you clean, thank God for His saving, cleansing work in the waters of Baptism.

The Good Ol' Days

Philippians 3:13–14

For many people, living in the past is fun. It allows them to relive highlights from the conference playoff game; cruising with their first love in their first car (for some, their first car was their first love); buying pants with a waist measurement smaller than the inseam; falling head over heels for a different girl each month; and getting an allowance without getting any bills in the mail. The past sounds awfully inviting at times.

For others, the past was filled with days that can hardly be described as good. Although they would rather not remember, their minds keep reliving memories of abuse, loneliness, abandonment, or fear.

Although it's easy, it's not wise or healthy to live in the past. If the good ol' days were truly good, those memories can create unrealistic expectations for today's relationships and situations. For those whose memories are filled with less-than-good ol' days, the memories can devastate.

There is one healthy, helpful way to live in the past. It can enhance your present days while moving you into the future with confidence. To move forward we need to *daily* go back to a day described as "good." It was a Friday called Good. Each day we need to relive, rejoice in, and be revived by the memories and truth of that day—in fact, that entire holy weekend.

At the crossroads outside the city wall of Jerusalem, we find a healthy direction for our present lives. At the cross we find forgiveness as Christ takes our sins upon Himself. We hear an invitation to leave our past hurts at the feet of our Savior as He heals us and leads us into healthier tomorrows. There we see the perfect, unconditional, sacrificial love of our Savior—an example of how we are to love one another. We go back to find our future, an eternal future that includes heaven. Through our Spirit-created faith in this Jesus, we have been made heirs of heaven's riches and the eternal blessings of paradise. No matter our past, we have a great future in Christ.

Father to Father: Father, for the joys of the good ol' days, I thank You. I unburden myself of the hurts I still carry from past days and give them to You as You have asked me to do. In the name of Jesus I pray and live. Amen.

God's Man in Action: Share your past with your children via your high school yearbook or photo albums. Then share with them Philippians 3:13–14 and tell them what it means to you to remember the past but move into the future with joy through Jesus.

Giving a Lift

1 Timothy 2:1

God's Word tells us to pray for one another. If you don't have a prayer list, use this as a starter. Since this book is written for fathers (and those who love them), this partial prayer list will focus on our needs as brothers in Christ. Let's lift each other up in prayer.

Let us pray for fathers who are

- out of work and for those who are out of control.
- raising stepchildren and for those raising the level of integrity in their lives.
- feeling overburdened and in need of giving their burdens to the Lord.
- building a new home and for those struggling to build a savings account.
- striving to imitate Christ and for those who are not intimate with their wives.
- coping with thoughts of divorce and for those who are coping after divorce.
- in physical pain and for those trying to keep from causing physical pain.

- grieving a loss and for those who rejoice at learning of God's promise of eternal life.
- dealing with aging and others who are dealing with aging parents.
- feeling lost and our brothers who seem to have lost compassionate feelings.
- honoring their wives and families and in turn are honoring God.
- growing in their faith and others who are dying because of lack of faith.
- ministering to other families and families who are ministering to fathers.
- traveling on business and for those who are busy traveling back to God's ways.
- not able to see their children and for children who don't know their fathers.
- expecting a child and those expecting other miracles.
- battling diseases or handicaps and for all fathers battling the disease of sin.
- short on patience and for those who are doctors treating patients.
- learning to worship in Spirit and truth and for those who have difficulty telling the truth.
- burdened by guilt and for those who are freed by God's forgiveness.
- behind prison walls and for those who are living in sin-imposed prisons.

- putting work before God and family and for those who are working at putting God first.
- addicted to substances and others who are working at a substantive friendship.
- dealing with the empty-nest syndrome and for those with an empty-heart syndrome.
- rejoicing in their children's accomplishments and for those who are accomplishing the joyful task of teaching their children to rejoice in all circumstances.
- in the middle of a midlife crisis and for those who are in the middle of a midday prayer.
- putting their children through school and for those who are putting themselves through school.
- teenagers and for those with teenagers.
- working daily on making their marriage work and for those who are looking for help in making their marriage work.
- praying and are strengthened by knowing others are praying for them.

Father to Father: Father, hear my prayers for other fathers and for myself. Send Your Son to intercede for fathers throughout the world. Amen.

God's Man in Action: Start your own prayer list for fathers or add to this one. Let us lift one another up in daily prayer.

A NOF Is Not Enough

Luke 5:16

O ur family had a NOF last Friday. NOF is new to our household, an idea from our friends. They have two sons and saw the value of spending one-on-one time with each child.

Each month they designate a night when each parent takes one of their sons out. The child makes the plans (within reason). Excitement is added by keeping the plans secret. It teaches planning skills and, possibly, financial responsibility, depending on the event. They honor their children by wanting to do things the children enjoy. The entire family anticipates these nights. The parent and child take time for each other, get to know each other, and create wonderful memories.

These "date nights" can consist of a variety of activities. It's important to let the child plan the outing. (I did step in when my sons planned to fly to Chicago.) It can be fun to picnic and play at the park, rent a video and order pizza in, play at a video arcade, take in a sporting event, go to the mall, or enjoy a hike. The ideas can come as fast as your children's minds can create them.

We loved the idea of this quality, fun time. We quickly added it to our calendar. We chose to name it NOF (Night of Fun). We recently had our first one. It was wonderful! With three children, we spend one-on-one and two-on-one time.

My wife, Chiara, said the best part of her evening with Sarah came on the way home when Sarah exclaimed excitedly, "I'll always remember this!" It was obvious that she treasured the personal attention of her mom. Similarly, I had a great time with the boys. We all are looking forward to next month's NOF.

A NOF is a very important experience. But a NOF is not enough if it's all there is to your relationship. Obviously, children crave time with their parents, but that time needs to be more than once a month. It may be an entire evening focused on them, but personal attention is a necessary component for a solid, healthy, and growing relationship.

This may mean putting down the newspaper when our children talk to us. We can turn off the computer to give full attention to helping them with their homework. We can look our children in the eyes when they talk to us. We can let them help us cook supper, even though it would be quicker and neater if we did it on our own. (Well, quicker—maybe not neater.) Sometimes sitting together in a hammock or a rocker without any distractions communicates the world to our children.

Children crave personal attention. They learn about

respecting other people's words and ways from how we respect, or fail to respect, their words and ways. As we keep our eyes fixed on Jesus Christ, we also focus on the concerns, joys, and needs of others.

We also need to realize that our heavenly Father plans one-on-one time with us, His children. He knows how we need and crave His attention. Jesus often withdrew to lonely places and prayed. He loved the time alone with His Father as much as our children love their one-on-one time with us. Jesus was strengthened during those times. He needed the strength to face the stress, crowds, antagonizing Pharisees, and all the demands of ministry and daily life. Through our time alone with our Father, we also receive strength to face the demands of life. We pass God's strength on to our children through our time alone with them and by teaching them to take one-on-one time with their heavenly Father.

Father to Father: I want to take more "alone" time with You, Father, to draw from Your love, wisdom, and strength. Thanks for Your love that lets me call You my Father through Jesus Christ. Amen.

God's Man in Action: Would a NOF be a nice monthly addition to your calendar and life?

Asking Directions

John 14:1–6

Most of us have heard the jokes about the male defective direction-asking gene. Question: "Why did it take Moses 40 years to lead the Israelites from Egypt to the Promised Land?" Answer: "Because he was a man and refused to ask directions."

Or: "Why does it take millions of male sperm to conceive a child but only one female egg?" Answer: "Because none of them will take the time to stop and ask directions."

See, our problems start even before we're conceived.

Let it be noted that there are many instances when dads have successfully assembled their children's toys without one glance at the instructions. Many families have arrived safely at their vacation destination (by the grace of God) without chauffeur Dad asking for directions at the gas station. And without wasting too much time (and a little pride), fathers have figured out how to play the latest video game without asking their children for assistance.

Yes, men have had many successful accomplishments that have been buried under a pile of failures.

(Our families keep score, in case you didn't know, but don't ask for it.)

There is one area in which men must never be bashful about putting the direction-asking gene to use. (By the way, the gene isn't defective, just unused.) God's Word calls for fathers to raise their children in the training and instruction of the Lord (Ephesians 6:4). What a responsibility! Fellow fathers, we are on a journey, with our wives, to lead our children up the Lord's road, which leads to heaven.

Jesus also gave a group of men directions to heaven. One of them, Thomas, doubted his direction gene. He decided to ask Jesus, His Lord, the way to where He was going (John 14:5).

The directions to heaven were presented in a clear and precise manner. Jesus said, "I am the way and the truth and the life. No one comes to the Father except through Me" (John 14:6). No turns, no detours, no other options. You can't miss it ... if you go through Jesus Christ. He is the only way to heaven. There are no alternate routes, period!

The directions are clear. Fathers, raise your children in the training and instruction of the Lord, which leads to heaven, through faith in Jesus Christ.

The Lord has graciously left us the instructions, training manual, and directions for our journey through this life in Him to life eternal with Him. I hope it isn't hidden in your home under two inches of dust, five unused road maps, and a pile of untouched instruction manuals for various games, appliances, and toys. I hope your Bible—God's book of directions—is readily accessible, worn from daily use, and parts can be found in your heart and on your lips.

In the Old Testament, godly parents were instructed to impress God's Word and ways on their children. They were to talk about Him when they sat at home, when they laid down to sleep, when they woke up in the morning, and when they traveled along the road (Deuteronomy 6:4–7). God's guidelines haven't changed. Our joyful calling is a constant responsibility.

I just had a thought: If we are to teach our children while traveling on the road, let's hope that we aren't lost while traveling. If we are trying to teach our children dependence on God, we should mirror that activity by depending on others to help us. It's okay and good to ask directions. In fact, true independence comes from dependence on God.

Father to Father: Thank You, Father, for the directions we need to lead our family home. I come to You, in prayer, through Jesus Christ. Amen.

God's Man in Action: Keep an extra Bible in your car—maybe in your glove compartment, next to the maps. Take time to read, learn, and teach the next time you travel.

My Daughter—the Heretic?

Psalm 32

We joined hands around the table as Sarah cleared her throat and prepared to take us to the throne room of God. "Thank You for this nice day and for school and for us being able to go outside and play. Thank You for this food. And thank You for dying on the cross and for saving our sins. Amen."

Wait a minute! I really don't want to say "Amen—so be it, Lord" to that last line of the prayer. Was I holding hands with a heretic? We got it straightened out. She had made an honest mistake. The absence of those two little words—*us* and *from*—make a big difference in the prayer and our lives.

My little heretic, I mean, daughter, meant to pray, "And thank You for dying on the cross and for saving *us from* our sins." Details, details. Actually, that's a detail that many people wouldn't notice because not only do they save their sins but they're certain that God is doing the same. Some people save stamps, others, baseball cards; still others save their sins. Let us also make it clear that God gracefully saves sinners, not the forgiven sins of the sinner.

Let's face facts, Jesus Christ came into the world to

save sinners (1 Timothy 1:15). He offers forgiveness of sins to His repentant children (1 John 1:8–9). If He kept a record of sins, who could stand (Psalm 130:3)? He says, "Their sins and lawless acts I will remember no more" (Hebrews 10:17) and "As far as the east is from the west, so far has He removed our transgressions from us" (Psalm 103:12).

Now let's "faith" the facts. God's Word shows us our sin and the one who forgives our sins. And in forgiving us, He doesn't save our sins, He forgets them. We need to sink our faith into these life-giving promises of our Savior. God does not save our sins. Neither should we.

David tried saving his sins. His story is dramatic. It is probably familiar because it strikes a chord in our lives. David recalls trying to save his sins and hide them deep inside his soul. He writes: "When I kept silent, my bones wasted away through my groaning all day long. For day and night Your hand was heavy upon me; my strength was sapped as in the heat of summer" (Psalm 32:3–4). I think we all have been there. The guilt haunts us. The truth of God's Word won't loosen its grip. We are worn out and in need of help. It doesn't work to save our sins. It's unhealthy. It has eternal consequences. It hurts God, us, and others.

David found help in God alone. He rejoiced, while encouraging fellow sinners, "Blessed is he whose transgressions are forgiven, whose sins are covered" (Psalm 32:1). He acknowledged his sin to God. He couldn't hide or save it any longer. And God forgave his sin and relieved the nagging guilt. David was freed to commit his ways to God.

It won't work for God our Father to hold our sins either. Jesus Christ has come to stand in our place before the Father. He covers our imperfect lives with His perfection. If we had to stand before God alone, we wouldn't have a chance. God has saved us—not our forgiven sins.

Sarah and I are grateful for our God who forgives and forgets our heretical sins and our hypocritical lives. His forgiveness and grace motivates us to turn away from our sins and follow closer in our Savior's perfect steps. Forgiven fathers, let us hold hands and pray—confessing our sins, seeking forgiveness for Jesus' sake. Let us also thank Him for *not* saving our sins but for saving *us from* our sins. Details! Details!

Father to Father: Pray a prayer of confession, thanksgiving, and commitment.

God's Man in Action: If you are holding onto a sin that someone has committed against you, release him or her and the sin by forgiving as you have been forgiven.

Dimples to Die For

Romans 5:12

During the first weeks of Christopher's life, Benjamin and Sarah saw it as their job to make their new baby brother smile and laugh. One day as Christopher was laughing, Benjamin said, "Look at his dimples." A few seconds later, when the laughing subsided, Benjamin said, "Oh look, he closed them now."

Christopher is constantly getting compliments on his dimples. One day in the mall, a lady seemed to covet them when she said, "Those are dimples to die for!" (A little extreme, I thought.) Smiling dimples are almost always seen as a great blessing.

When someone compliments Christopher on his dimples, I wonder if they know that they are actually anatomical flaws. Dimples are actually caused by a developmental flaw in the tissue that connects the skin to the bone. Rarely do flaws attract such positive comments as dimples do. Dimples can be very attractive, drawing the attention of many people.

In today's world, it seems that many flaws of sinful men and women are being praised as something good. The world seems to glorify sin, making it difficult for our children to know what is right and wrong. They are bombarded with mixed messages from television, music, classmates, and a very confused world. But children aren't the only ones affected.

As parents, we have passed our sinful flaws on to our children. All of us were conceived and born sinful (Psalm 51:5). Sin is a hereditary flaw we surely can't be proud of. It is something we will die for. Romans 5:12 says, "Therefore, just as sin entered the world through one man, and death through sin, and in this way death came to all men, because all sinned." Then the flawed, but inspired, Paul writes, "For the wages of sin is death" (Romans 6:23).

It is just another reminder that we need to know what God calls a sin and what He calls a blessing. We cannot take lightly our sin or the sins of those around us. We need to make sure that Satan's world isn't attracting us into a false truth that says what was once a sin is now something attractive. As parents, we have a tremendous responsibility to lovingly share both God's Law and His precious Gospel. God is deadly serious about sin.

He is just as serious about His gift of grace through Jesus Christ. We must not take that lightly either.

Romans 6:23 opens with talk of death, but it closes with this good news truth, "But the gift of God is eternal life in Christ Jesus our Lord." Christ's perfection covers our flaws as, by the Spirit's guidance, we live for Him who died for us. Our sinful flaws bring death, but Jesus brings life.

It doesn't surprise me that God can take a flaw such as a dimple and open it up into an attractive and desirable feature. He has a wonderful habit of doing that. But it also doesn't surprise me that Satan and sinful humanity can take sin and turn it into something attractive. Yet all the while, it is something to die for.

It is grace that caused Jesus Christ to see my many sinful flaws yet make the life-giving decision that I was someone to die for. He took a cross of death that the world would see as a curse and turned it into a place of life.

When I look at Christ Crucified and Christ Ever-living, it makes me smile and show my dimples as I say, "Now there's Someone to live for!"

Father to Father: In Jesus my sinful flaws have been covered perfectly. Teach me to pass that truth (and all Your truths) on to my family, Father, as we live for You. Amen.

God's Man in Action: See how many smiling dimples you notice today. As you do, be thankful for the smiles and recall God's truth about our sinful flaws and His perfect grace in Jesus Christ.

A Week in God's Creation

Genesis 1:1–2:3

In the beginning was Monday morning in this home that God created. As the alarm rang, any thoughts toward movement were absent as my supply of motivation was at an all-time low. The Spirit of God was hovering but went unnoticed. I said, "Let there be hot water left for my shower." And, surprisingly, there was, but that was not the only hot water I would get into that day. There was morning and evening, the first day of a week that I hoped would not act as a foretaste of things to come.

On the second day someone said, "Let there be some reason for your actions." There was none (that they approved of). That was morning. Evening proceeded in a similar fashion.

The sun rose on the third day and so did the level of the voices in our house. Tempers were short, and no one was long on patience. All creation was stirring. I yelled, "Let there be silence!" But there was none.

The next day, the officer said, "Let me see your license, sir. You were speeding." There was none, for I had left it on my dresser. My heart was speeding faster than my car had been as I considered the outcome. As far as the ticket, I saw that it was not good. I was still in mourning when I came home that evening.

The fifth day came and went as all the rest. I begged, "Let there be a way out of this rut." But there didn't seem to be any alternatives. I dodged pot holes as I rode through the rest of the day with two tires in the gutter.

The sixth day brought road maps for shuttle service to activities, game plans for uncharted chores, and hopes for a date with my mate that never materialized. Morning seemed like a fading memory as evening came accompanied by exhaustion.

Then came the seventh day of the week in God's creation. On that day I desperately needed rest. So I went to church with my family. On that day God breathed into my life the fragrant scent of His life-giving love. He formed out of the dust on my Bible an inscription that read: "Let My Word be a lamp to your feet and a light to your path as you journey in My creation." He walked me through passage after passage. I stopped. He expounded. I reflected.

He pointed me to those sitting around me whom He had sent to help me through the week. I had failed to notice them. He reminded me of the blessings He sent this week that I had ignored. He explained that when I was complaining, He was opening doors of opportunities to witness.

I confessed to God how I had created a mess out of His week in creation. Then He led me to His altar.

There I tasted of His forgiveness, and He strengthened my faith through a meal He calls His own. Then He led me out of His house and into mine, blessed and refreshed.

It was very good! It was all very good news to me, His new creation.

The Lord God had created in me a new, willing, and steadfast spirit. He had restored to me the joy of my salvation, which is mine through Christ Jesus. It was a holy day of rest to rejoice in. It had been a holy day and week. When I was weak, He gave His strength so I could join with all creation in singing His eternal praise.

Father to Father: Father, I join all of Your creation, praising You for Your goodness and grace. Create in me, Your new creation, a new, willing, and steadfast spirit today. May this coming Sunday (and all the days of the week) be a true day of resting in Your arms of love. In Jesus' name I bring these petitions to Your throne. Amen.

God's Man in Action: Make a spreadsheet with seven columns. Fill the columns with various ways you have witnessed God working in your days. Pray that this week of blessings will strengthen you in your weak days.

Take Two Tablets and Call Me in the Mourning

Exodus 20:1–17

When it comes to rules, parents often come out looking like the bad guys. We hear the "But, Dad!" followed by long faces and dejected spirits. If you're like me, I find myself feeling as though I have to justify the rules my wife and I established in love for our children.

But in the next moment I can find myself as the child—of God. Handing me the tablets of the Law, my heavenly Father says, "Take these two tablets and call me in the mourning." The Ten Commandments were given in love by the Father to His children. As I examine the tablets of the Law, I find myself in mourning for I have terribly failed my Father and the people around me.

Join me in taking the tablets (of Law) and holding them up to our lives—as men of God and as fathers who are leaving a legacy to our children. God's Law will leave us mourning our failures.

One: Loving or trusting someone or something more than God. Is it children, wife, job; self?

Two: Respect our Father's holy name. What are

we teaching our children about respecting God's name, will, and Word?

Three: Regular private and corporate worship is a must. Are the psalmist's words our words? "I rejoiced with those who said to me, 'Let us go to the house of the LORD.'" (Psalm 122:1).

Four: Here's a parent's favorite—show respect for those in authority. How do we show our children that we respect our parents and all others in authority? Do we also honor our children?

Five: Do not hurt someone physically. Is your temper under control? Have we broken this command by not supporting our neighbor in every physical need?

Six: Job had the right idea: "I made a covenant with my eyes not to look lustfully at a girl" (Job 31:1). See how Jesus backed up this command in Matthew 5:27–28.

Seven: Do not steal. Not a problem? How often this week have we stolen time from God? Do we think work won't miss the paper clips? Do we rob from God in our offerings and tithes (Malachi 3:8)?

Eight: It's a myth that men don't gossip. Do we fail to put the best construction on situations?

Nine and Ten: Do not covet. But what about those petty jealousies of the possessions, lifestyle, or even the family of another.

That's just a taste of the tablets. When we call on God in mourning over our sins, we come confessing them. We come in sincere repentance. *Repentance* means turning 180 degrees away from, in this case, our sins. We turn away from them to follow in God's perfect ways, which are the opposite direction from Satan's destructive path.

When we call on God, in repentance, He recalls His Son, Jesus, who lived under the tablets of the Law and kept them perfectly in our place. He recalls His Son, who rose in the morning, amidst the mourning. He broke through the mourning with news of victory over sin, Satan, and death. When we call on Him in our mourning, He reminds us that He has called us by name, claimed us as His own, and saved us by His Son's suffering, death, and resurrection. Through Christ we have forgiveness from the laws we have broken.

Take two tablets (of Law) and call on Him in the mourning. The Son of God rose in the mourning and brings us into the light of His forgiving grace.

Father to Father: Forgive me, Father, for I have sinned. Instead of sitting in mourning all day, I run to You for forgiveness and grace in my time of need. At the cross, Your Son covers me with His life. Today is this dad's day in the Son. (By the way, I'll need the Son tomorrow too. And the next day ...) Amen.

God's Man in Action: Examine the Ten Commandments and your life. Confess your sin and receive God's forgiveness as He empowers you to live your day in the Son. When you see an aspirin bottle, take the tablets of the Law to heart and swallow with a sip of God's grace.

I'm Telling

Matthew 28:18–20

Is there a statistics book on children? If there is, one of the first things I'd like to check is how many times the average child says, "I'm telling!"

My children, who are presently in a "telling" stage, probably would throw the average off. (It's been a three-year stage.) They always seem to tell the bad news. I can only imagine the day when I hear, "Dad, she was being polite to me. She helped me and told me how she liked my picture. She even gave me a hug. I just thought you'd want to know, Dad." (It's okay to dream, isn't it?)

A telling stage isn't all bad, depending on what you're telling.

The story of Jesus Christ is a telling one. God told Adam and Eve. The prophets told God's people. Gabriel told Mary. Angels told the shepherds. The shepherds told everyone they met. The Holy Spirit told Simeon. The Magi told Herod. John the Baptizer told those in the desert. Jesus told fishermen, tax collectors, and many others. Philip told Nathaniel. The newly healed told their families. People told the Pharisees. The Pharisees told Herod. Herod told the crowd. Jesus told the thief on the cross. The Holy Spirit told the centurion. The angel told the women. The women told the disciples. Jesus told His followers walking to Emmaus. Jesus told Thomas. And the angel told the sky-gazing disciples just after Jesus told the disciples to go and tell everyone everything about Himself.

The telling story doesn't stop there. The Bible told me, as did my mother, Sunday school teachers, Christian day school teachers, and many others. I've told my children. I've told the congregations I've served. I'm in the process of telling you. That's the power of God's Word and His Gospel.

No doubt about it—the story of Jesus Christ is a telling one. But if statistics were revealed, I imagine there is more listening to the story than telling it. How many times have you heard the story of Jesus Christ, the world's Savior? How often have you told it?

The story of God's salvation plan—Jesus' birth, life, death, resurrection, and ascension—is a story to behold. But God's salvation story is also a story to be told and retold and retold.

It's a privilege for each of us to share this telling story of the one called Jesus. Jesus told His first disciples and He tells us, His modern disciples, to tell the world—starting at home.

If you're going to say you're uneasy telling others because you don't have a master's in communications, fear not! The Master can communicate through you. He will tell His masterfully told story not only through your words, but also in your Christ-like acts of humility, love, and childlike faith. Whom did He use to tell His story in the first place? Sinners and saints, angels and archangels, uneducated shepherds and unsuspecting merchants, the rich and the poor, teenagers and teachers, moms and dads. Isn't that telling you something wonderful? God loves to hear His people say, "I'm telling!"

You have a household, a neighborhood, and a workplace that need to hear His story—a world of sinners who need to know their forgiving Savior. They need to know the hope that is found in the story of Jesus' life, death, and resurrection for them. They need to know of His love. And God wants to use you and me to tell them all His telling story of salvation. Think where you'd be if no one had told you.

That does it: I'm telling! How about you?

Father to Father: Father, I'm so grateful for those who have told me Your story. Make me a useful instrument to tell others of Your love and life—starting at home. In the name of Jesus. Amen.

God's Man in Action: Tell your children today what Jesus Christ means to you. Tell them who some of the first people were to tell you His story.

An Omelet and Side Dish to Go

Genesis 3:17–19

While I was on vacation, I visited with a fellow father. He was serving me a late breakfast while my family was swimming in the pool next to my restaurant table. This father served up more than an omelet and orange juice. He also served up a nice side dish to go. It was a mixture of compliments, reflections, and advice.

As I ate, we conversed. It began as he complimented me on my family. He said that he had been blessed with a wife and two sons, ages 12 and 19. He proudly told me that his older son was attending a local university with plans to be a lawyer. Although he was obviously proud of both sons, the accomplishment of this son was a special joy.

He proceeded to tell me that he had grown up in a very poor family in Mexico. He did not have the opportunity for much schooling. There were coconut trees nearby, and his job was to cut and sell the fruit. A few animals provided a little additional income. His son's accomplishments proved to be a crowning jewel in his life experience.

He was happy to have provided a roof and food for his family. Even though his income was meager, he had provided his son with an opportunity. He was thankful that his son had seized it.

Then this father (who was about 10 years my senior) served up some advice hidden in the form of a personal regret. He shared that when his children were younger, he had not taken his role of father and provider seriously. Now that he was more mature, he realized the importance of family, their well-being, and working toward future goals. Although his firstborn was attending college, he had the hope that his other son would follow. As he watched my family playing in the water, he shared his final thought. "Family is very important."

By that time my plate was empty, and I was down to my last sip of juice. I was thankful for the meal but more appreciative of the conversational side dish. I was happy that we could share as fathers, and I was thankful for his family's victorious journey.

What a blessing that two strangers could share in the gift and responsibility of family. It's the first time I ate at a restaurant where the waiter left me a tip.

Even though we live in an age where both parents often share the role of provider, I think most men feel the greater burden of that responsibility. I guess it goes back to the conversation God served up to Adam after he had finished chewing on the forbidden fruit (Genesis 3:17–19).

It is a blessing to be able to leave our children more than what we had. Yet that will not always be the scenario. The most important gift our children can have is a solid, Spirit-created faith in Jesus Christ on which they can live and grow. Faith is a gift of God, not man-made or a parent hand-me-down. But God, the perfect Provider, Protector, and Preserver, wants to work through us within the lives of our families.

No matter the experience or financial situation in which our children will live as adults, their spiritual foundation is of utmost importance. When they're founded on Christ, we know they will always be rich, no matter their checkbook balance. They are heirs of the riches of heaven. One day the curse will be lifted and only eternal blessings will remain.

Father to Father: Father, the provisions You made for me are eternal. By Your Spirit, work through me to provide the necessities of life for my children. In Jesus' name. Amen.

God's Man in Action: Drop a dollar or two into your children's piggy banks or savings accounts. Then drop a prayer or two into the ear of your providing Father who has promised to hear and answer. That is something you can bank on.

Father Abraham

Genesis 22:1–19

Dad, I remember the day like it was yesterday. You woke me up early and said we were going on a trip. You were skimpy on the details. Then again, you were quite unpredictable, so I looked forward to an adventure.

It didn't take long to notice something was on your mind. Your quietness made me uneasy. You seemed to want to say something but didn't know how. I wondered if something awful was happening to you or Mom. Then I got scared.

I recalled the nights you would go off to pray. You were gone so long. It was obvious you had a heavy heart. You didn't know this, but on the second night I followed you. From a distance, I watched you. You prayed, and then you looked up at the star-filled sky. You seemed to be counting them. Then you prayed some more.

On the third day, I realized that the wood you asked me to carry would soon be my bed. I remember asking about a lamb for the sacrifice. We had everything but a lamb.

I didn't realize at the time how insightful, faith-driven, and even prophetic your answer was. "God Himself will provide the lamb for the burnt offering, my son," you said. I trusted you as you trusted God. Thank you for that gift of trust.

Were those tears or sweat running down your face as we built the altar? I assumed they were drops of sweat, but now I wonder if I was wrong. When you started to bind me, I remember asking, "Why are you doing this, Father?" You kept repeating, "I love you. Trust me. Trust the Lord." Today my question is, "How could you, Father? How did you have the faith and trust to listen to a God who told you to sacrifice your own son?" I don't know if I could do that.

When you lifted the knife above my throat, I didn't know whether to cry or laugh. If this was a joke, I didn't see the humor in it. You seemed to hesitate as though you were waiting for something or someone to intercede. When I heard the voice of the angel, I realized that this was no joke. God had asked you to do the impossible, and you loved Him more than you loved me. I respect you for that. I truly do.

I can say with the angel what I already knew for years, "I know that you fear God." Most everything you did told me that you stood in awe of God. Reflecting on it, all the loose ends seem to come together. God had promised you and Mom that your offspring would be as numerous as the stars in the sky. You knew God was faithful to all His promises. You trusted Him. I was a star, wasn't I? I was a star that had fallen from God's heaven into your lap. You knew He could fill a sky with me and the numbers of your offspring.

Dad, the Lord used you as a wonderful teacher of powerful lessons. I had much to learn. You taught me to love and trust God for all things and above all things—even family. You taught me that if the Lord blesses me with children, I will have to make sacrifices for the Lord's sake, which will also be for their sakes. He has our best interest in mind. I have learned from you that God is faithful to all His promises. My instruction brought me to the point of realizing that God will never test us beyond what we can handle. He will never ask for a sacrifice from us without providing the gift. This time it was a ram. Next time it could be the blood of the Lamb of God that He will provide for our sacrifice.

I love you, Father. You are my inspiration.

Your son, Isaac.

Father to Father: Grant me the faith and love of Father Abraham. I pray this in the name of the Lamb You provided as the perfect sacrifice for my sins. Amen.

God's Man in Action: Study and reflect on Genesis 12:1–9; 15:1–5; 22:1–15.

Getting Small

Matthew 18:2

The bath water was draining. The toothbrushes had their workout. Bladders had been emptied. It must be bedtime. That summer night the thermometer was pushing 95. The air conditioner was pushing even harder. Benjamin picked the bedtime story—the birth of Jesus.

We were six months away from Christmas. My first thought was to urge him to pick another. (It was the adult in me.) Okay, why not? Any time is a good time to remember God's most precious gift—His Son. Warm up those angel choirs (they can compete with the hum of the air conditioner) and let's go to Bethlehem.

Somewhere between Mary wrapping the baby in swaddling clothes and the visit of the shepherds, Benjamin had a 5-year-old question filled with lessons for a 30-something dad.

"How does Jesus get small again every Christmas?"

Where was Solomon when I needed wisdom? (Where was my wife for that matter?) It wasn't that difficult a question actually. "No, son, He doesn't get small again every Christmas. He was only a child once. Now let's get back to the shepherds." We returned to the flock of sheep, but the question stuck with me until my bedtime.

Each year, just before Christmas we pretend that Jesus isn't here yet. He is born and He's small again. Like faithful parents we nurse Him, rather quickly, through His life that spanned 30-something years. But according to the church calendar, it only took four or five months. We watch Him grow, and we beam proudly when He puts the Pharisees to shame. We brag about His miracles. We cry with Him at Lazarus' tomb. Then our hearts almost break in two as we stand at the foot of His cross with His mother. We nurse the Christmas child along through His life and ministry. Then it's back in the womb, just in time for Advent. He becomes a child again, and we relive His joys and agonies year after year.

Maybe I should have given Benjamin a different answer. "In one way Jesus does get small again every Christmas. Maybe He does it to teach us to get small again every Christmas and to stay there throughout the year."

Do you remember Christmas as a child? For me, it was a magical kingdom of fun and excitement, wonder, and awe. The spirit and the tree were real. I could smell the hay. Through the voices of carolers, a multitude of heavenly hosts was right outside the door. Gifts were surprises received in love rather than a fulfillment of an obligation.

Oh, to get small again every Christmas and to stay

there throughout the year. Oh, to listen to the Master Teacher preach on the mount or to hear Him through a frail vessel from a pulpit. Oh, to be filled with a child's awe at every miracle rather than taking them for granted. Oh, to be horrified, like a child, as our best friend in the whole world is nailed to a cross because He loves us. And then to dance with childlike glee, with tears of joy, at the sight of the empty tomb where He calls out our name.

With a child next to Him, Jesus once said, "Unless you change and become like little children, you will never enter the kingdom of heaven" (Matthew 18:3). Martin Luther echoed that thought for parents, saying that if we are to bring up children, we must become children with them. My son's question reminded me to get small again on that hot summer evening. It was time for me to lay my inhibitions aside and lay my treasured gifts at the Christ Child's feet.

Father to Father: Bring out the Child in me, Father. Allow Him to stay as I unwrap His "presence" every day of the year. In the name of the Christ Child, I pray. Amen.

God's Man in Action: Be creative and celebrate Christmas with your family tonight. Luke 2:1–20 is a great bedtime story any day of the year—for God's children of all ages.

A "Lot" to Consider

Psalm 16

C liché or not, the grass often is greener on the other side. Sometimes that's the case because it's artificial turf.

Do you spend time looking at your neighbor's lot? Do you envy his family sitting on a lush green yard where things seem perfect? What's the difference between your lot and his?

"How are you—how's life?" If everyone answered that question openly and honestly, we would have fewer people asking. Consider the following questions: "How's fatherhood? How's your home life? How's life at work? How's life treating you?" Answer those questions in your mind with complete honesty. My prayer is that your answers are filled with great things.

Realistically, there probably are regrets, frustrations, and concerns in most areas of our lives. It seems as though the majority of people are dissatisfied with their circumstances.

David gives us a lot to consider about life in Psalm 16. "Lord, You have assigned me my portion and my cup; You have made my lot secure. The boundary lines have fallen for me in pleasant places; surely I have a delightful inheritance" (Psalm 16:5–6).

David has the right focus in reviewing his life and situation. What if we changed the questions to "How's life in Christ?" and "How is the Lord treating you?" When the Lord enters the picture, the grass on our lot looks different.

I walked around the lot on which our house is built. I walked the fence that marked the boundary lines. It's not a perfect lot—in fact, the backyard is quite oddly shaped. Within the boundary lines, I saw our house and my beautiful family. There were blooming flowers mixed with weeds. There were play areas, rest areas, and also areas that needed quite a bit of work. There was a garage for our car (and lots of stuff), but there was also garbage that needed to be removed. It was all together on my lot.

As I consider my lot as a Christian husband, father, and child of God, I see areas of beauty along with areas of failure and sin. I notice the boundary lines. They start at the baptismal font, as God brought me into His family. Then the lines move outward when I walked from His will. Then He brought me back, close to Him again, as He led me down His path. There were failures followed by forgiveness. I suddenly realized that the boundary lines of my life had fallen in delightful places. The lines were in the shape of a cross.

Christ's life, death, and resurrection covered my life perfectly. He had provided a delightful inheritance for me and my family. His inheritance was in the form of forgiveness and "foreverness," power and peace, joy in Jesus, purpose and pleasure, compassion and companionship.

As men of God, we have a lot to consider when we think about the "lot" with which we have been blessed. The Lord has led us into the greenest of pastures. He has provided an eternal inheritance that cannot fade, rust, or be stolen. Yes, we have a lot to work on, but we also have a lot to be thankful for.

Father to Father: Gracious Dad, I have a lot to be thankful for. Keep me gazing on the green pastures You have led me to graze on. Help me make the necessary improvements. What a joy it is to be a father under Your divine guidance. In Jesus' name I come to You. Amen.

God's Man in Action: Take a walk around the lot on which you live. Note the beauty and the areas that need work. Compare it to the lot in life that God has laid out for you.

All I Need

1 Corinthians 2:2

Robert Fulghum wrote a charming personal credo a few years back that has become very popular. It not only has found its way to refrigerator doors but also to best-seller lists under the title *All I Ever Needed to Know I Learned in Kindergarten*. His thoughts were insightful, amusing, and delightful. It stated that all he really needed to know about how to live, what to do, and how to be, he learned in kindergarten.

It would be a great blessing if our children could one day write a similar credo titled *What I Really Need to Know I Learned from My Christian Father*. With that in mind, I will take out my poetic license and add a sequel to Fulghum's piece.

- Most of what I really needed to know about how to live—and what to do and how to be—I learned from my Christian father. Wisdom was not at the top of the graduate school mountain but in the sixth pew on the pulpit side where I sat next to my father in church each week. It was also in the garage where he taught me about creating birdhouses and values. Life-wisdom was also found within my father's car where we shared jokes and laughter, our stories and Bible stories.

- These are some things I learned (even if I didn't fully understand them at the time) from my Christian father: Share with others what God has shared with you. Respect others as you want to be respected. Give thanks. Play. Pray. Spend as much time praying as you do playing. Smile and laugh— a lot. Take 10 (commandments as a guide). Repent. Know God and His grace intimately. Rejoice! Forgive. It's okay (and good) to admit a wrong. Love your child's mother. Have an attitude—patterned after the attitude of Jesus. Live the Lord's Prayer.

- When I go out without my father, I remember that my other Father is always with me. When I go out with my fathers, I hold their hands tightly.

- I recall the feeling of laying in my father's arms at night, his aftershave scent, and the touch of his scratchy cheek against mine. I learned from that and hold that memory tightly too.

- There were times on the ball field when the statistic book noted I struck out. That wasn't the case in my father's book. He's a great coach, even from the bleachers.

- My father read me devotions about Abraham, John, Paul, and Jesus. They all died. So will we, someday. But we will join them—still living—thanks to the latter.

- There is a story my father read from the Book about a cross and empty tomb that had the biggest word I had ever heard—*love!* Everything I need to know is somewhere in that word.

- All I really need to know I learned from my father because my father daily teaches me by living and sharing everything he knows about Jesus Christ.

This would be a wonderful gift from our children who see Christ's reflection in our lives. Earthly fathers are never perfect models. There is only one of those.

The apostle Paul also had an important credo. Unfortunately, it isn't as well-known or followed as Robert Fulghum's. It simply reads, "For I resolved to know nothing while I was with you except Jesus Christ and Him crucified" (1 Corinthians 2:2). What a great credo for us to live as a gift for our children.

Father to Father: Teach me, Father, to model Your life as my children model mine. I resolve to know Christ Crucified in my life and love. Through Christ I come to You. Amen.

God's Man in Action: Consider lifestyle changes that need to be made for you to know and live Christ Crucified. Take up the fun challenge to write a personal credo.

Intensive Care

Mark 15:33–37

One Friday afternoon I was called to intensive care. I joined a family with their loved one. Near death, he was in pain but never complained. His words were few.

The time passed slowly. It became a waiting game. There was nothing we could do. We tried to console one another. The dying man even tried to console us. As he spoke his last words and wishes, it became increasingly difficult for him to breathe. As I looked around at the friends and family who had gathered, it seemed everyone was trying to breathe for him.

We tried our best not to notice what was happening. Death is hard to ignore. We wished his hands weren't constrained. They played such a vital part in his life. His touch had once meant so much to so many. And now in his final hours of life, he couldn't move his hands.

One of the most difficult moments was when this man's own father walked out. He simply said, "I must leave." The dying man seemed to ache all the more with the absence of his father.

When there was silence, it seemed to last an eternity. Unexpected thunder and lightning startled us.

Actually it wasn't as quiet as we thought. It was a busy place, but we had blocked it out. Nearby, there were others facing the same outcome. The attendants talked among themselves. They seemed to be in charge, but who, except God, can be in charge of living and dying? The hours passed. And so did our friend. We watched him breathe his last.

God was in charge that day. And no matter how strange this may sound, it was a good day. As I think back on those unforgettable hours, I realize it was a very good day. It was a good Friday.

As my mind replays the events of that day, there is another aspect I will never forget. Intensive caring and love stand out in my mind during that vivid weekend. I will never forget that time because it didn't take place in a hospital intensive care unit. It took place last year, on Good Friday, as God's Word called me to a time and place of "intensive care." As I participated in the Good Friday Service of Darkness at church, I slipped into the surroundings. I stood at my Savior's feet with His family and friends. As I already noted, it is never easy to watch someone die.

But it is important to answer the call of our Savior, from the cross, to join Him as He breathes His last. The call is to witness the most intensive caring you have ever experienced. It is uncomfortable at times because your sin and mine have condemned this man to death. But at His death bed, made of wood, this dying Jesus shares His intense love for us and the entire world.

The caring is intensive and extensive. It is there, in death, that He hands us life, even though His hands have been confined by Roman nails. There He touches us with good news. There—amidst the living and dying, between family and friends, among those attending to His needs—there we find blood shed to give us life. Though pinned to a tree with all the sins of the world, He offers forgiveness. As His lungs are emptied, He fills us with the breath of life.

God is in charge. His graceful fingerprints mark His presence. He had planned this day of intensive care ever since an off-limits tree was invaded. It is God's Friday. It is a "good" Friday for us—for all who believe. This Father abandoned His Son on the cross to win for us peace, forgiveness, and the promise to never abandon us. The weekend and the news keep getting better as the hours pass. The crucified Jesus descended into hell to proclaim victory over sin and its master, Satan. And then there's Sunday. We are again called to an "intensive care" situation. The one whose hands were once confined walks past the stone that cannot hold back His life or love.

Father to Father: How good that Friday was! It makes all my days great. I thank You for Your intensive care as I am called to care intensely for You and my family. In the name of the one who suffered, died, and rose. Amen.

God's Man in Action: Cut a small cross out of thick cardboard. Carry it with you to remind you of the intensive caring of Christ Crucified, who will never leave you.

Delete Delight

1 Peter 4:8

Ever wish you had a "delete" key for certain situations, hours, and even entire days? It's so easy on a computer. You simply put your finger on the mouse. Click and drag the cursor across a word, sentence, or paragraph that you want removed. Then hit "delete." It's gone. Removed. Vanished. Then you're able to insert what you desire in place of what's been removed.

Today was a day I'd like to erase—most of it, anyway. I would love to start over. Waking up on time, when my three alarm clocks told me to, would be a nice start. Going to bed on time the night before would have been an even better start. After a short night of sleep, waking up in a panic and running late for an appointment is no fun. I was frustrated at myself for undersleeping and oversleeping.

Of course, being in a hurry means things take twice as long. I ran out the door leaving family hugs and kisses behind. My stomach reminded me that breakfast was missed. It notified my head, which decided to side with the stomach and punish me with a headache that aspirin couldn't conquer. God sent a downpour of rain even though He knew I hadn't brought an umbrella or raincoat.

I think you get the idea of how my day started. Imagine many more aggravating situations and insert them in the following hours before I arrived back home. Frustration, exhaustion, stress, anger, and a pounding headache accompanied me into my house. The worst part of the day was about to come.

Satan's allies, which had just escorted me through the door, led me to be short with my children. I yelled at them when it wasn't in any way necessary. Patience went flying out the window, along with wisdom and joy. Increased frustration took its place. My wife also was having a less-than-perfect day and wasn't feeling well. We were like two high-pressure systems meeting. It was raining outside and a storm watch was in effect on the inside. It had the potential of including high winds and rising *temper*atures.

It wasn't a good day. I wished I could start over. Where is the delete key when you need it? I took some time out and ended up inside our church. I sat in the pew and prayed.

Christ put His finger on the problem and on my heart, moving me to confess all that I had done wrong. Then His finger pointed me to His cross as He hit "delete." My sins were removed. Vanished. The patience, wisdom, and joy that had gone flying out the window of my house came flying in though His church's stained-glass window. It covered me, along with His forgiveness and grace. He allowed me to start again and insert in my life those actions, words, and thoughts that He desires as He lives within me.

It's amazing what confession and forgiveness can do for a soul, for a day, for a family. It was time to make the rounds. The first stop was my wife. She granted me her forgiveness. Next stop, my children—one at a time. I wanted to look them in the eye without distractions. When I called my daughter into my room, her first words were "What did I do?" I told her it was something Daddy did. I asked if she would forgive me for not being patient and for raising my voice at her. Without a thought, she gave me the gift I needed. She wrapped it in a bow shaped like a hug and sealed it with a kiss. My sons did the same.

A forgiving, unconditional love certainly does cover a multitude of sins. Now where's the "save" key? I want to add it to the overflowing file I've titled "Awesome Grace."

Father to Father: Frustration, lack of patience, and anger often accompany me, Father. Restore to me the joy of Your salvation and forgiveness. Just as I am, I come to You. Make me to be just as You are. In Jesus' name I pray. Amen.

God's Man in Action: Don't put off asking someone for the gift of forgiveness. If you use a computer, put a cross on the delete key as a reminder of God's forgiveness.

Mister Mom?

J an Frans, a Christian wife, mother of two, and author, wrote a tribute to dads that I found in a ministry magazine. She began by commenting that she noticed quite a contrast between messages in churches on Mother's Day and those shared on Father's Day. Mothers receive emotional words for their tenderness and sacrifices. Dads usually get a small note of appreciation, followed by a list of challenges on how to be more of a man. Jan thinks that wives often don't fully appreciate their husbands as fathers because they expect them to be male moms who parent exactly as they do.

She wrote to her women readers, "Really, girls, let's give these guys a break! Think about it: In the scope of eternity, what does it matter if our child's shirt or dress is dirty or wrinkled when Dad got them ready for church? Or, if they slept with their supper dried on their face after Dad put them to bed the night before? So what if Dad didn't insist they change their underwear before school for the third day in a row!? Won't the children forget the messy mouth, dirty shirt, and dingy drawers and instead remember the dad who was there? And who cares if the kids lost some sleep because Dad wrestled with them right before bed so they went from tired to wired? Will they not forget the fatigue and remember only the fun?"

Jan, on behalf of fathers everywhere, we thank you and shout, "Amen, sister!"

As I reread this article, I thought of a recent incident. A friend called to ask if I'd like to take my three children and meet him and his three children at a local ice-cream parlor while our wives attended a meeting. It sounded like a great idea to me—six children, two dads, and ice cream!

We arrived at the restaurant first. Soon, we saw their van pull into the parking lot. (By the way, I will be using an alias name to protect the reputation of a great father who had a brief lapse of paternal character.) Dan (wink, wink) opened the van door and two children hopped out. He held their hands and, with great parental care, led them to the door where we were waiting. We could almost hear the ice cream calling our names. Everything was set—two dads, ice cream, and five children.

Wait a minute, weren't there supposed to be *six* children? Where was Samantha (not her real name)? We looked out the restaurant window. There she was, sitting in her car seat, eyeing us from the van. Dan had left his youngest daughter in the van. Personally, I think it was ice cream on the brain. When I told my wife this story, I repeatedly reminded her that *I* did very well on the outing. She listened while holding our son's shirt, which appeared to be mostly chocolate ice cream. Okay, I forgot napkins, but at least I remembered the kids.

What is it about us guys? We try. We really do. We're not mothers (although they make mistakes too). We are fathers who love our children (and ice cream). Patience is a virtue that our wives need to obtain not only in dealing with children but also with us, God's children. Praise God for wives.

Thanks again for the encouragement found in your article, Jan. And thank You, God, for women in our lives who may not be named Grace but who exhibit that quality in dealing with us men. Thank You also for Your graceful ways and for never forgetting us, Your children.

Father to Father: Thank You for grace-filled, understanding women in our lives, Lord. Amen. *P.S.* Thank You also for Dan (wink, wink) and ice-cream runs.

God's Man in Action: Anyone in your family hungry for ice cream? Road trip time!

Dear Mom

2 Corinthians 3:2–3

M en learn a lot about being a father from their dads. But don't forget the parental instructor most of us had called Mom. Shortly before Mother's Day some years ago, I wrote a letter to my mother. She has had such a powerful influence on my life, faith, and parenting skills.

Dear Mom,

Mother's Day is just around the corner so I thought I'd write you a letter. I often think about your letters. I never knew a more prolific letter writer. Somehow you always found time to write. When I was away from home, I could count on at least one letter a week, often more. When I was home, I can still picture you sitting on the sofa with your writing tablet ... letter after letter after letter.

I don't know if I ever thanked you for all your letters. They were appreciated. It was always good to hear from home. Even if there wasn't all that much news, you'd find some.

The Cardinals and Cubs are tied 3–3 in the bottom of the sixth. They're taking the pitcher out! It doesn't make sense! They always take them out too early! ... Mrs. Wallgardner from church is in the hospital. You probably don't know her. ... Now the Cardinals are losing—I knew they took him out too early! ... The grass needs mowing and it's supposed to rain. I probably won't get it cut. ... The Cardinals lost—I knew it! Not much news, so I guess I'll go to bed.

Love, Mom.

Thanks for all the letters, Mom. I mean *all* the letters. That includes the ones you didn't write with your hands in your familiar hand-writing and style. It's the other ones that I most appreciate—the ones I'll never forget. Paul wrote and told me about them. "You yourselves are our letter, written on our hearts, known and read by everybody. You show that you are a letter from Christ ... written not with ink but with the Spirit of the living God, not on tablets of stone but on tablets of human hearts" (2 Corinthians 3:2–3).

Mom, the details of your handwritten let-ters may be forgotten, but the letters you allowed God to write through you, not on paper but through Christ living in you, will not be lost. I've got them stored in my heart. Christ's handwriting, compassionate style, and personal touch were in everything you did. Today I also thank God for the letters He has written to me through you. I see God's letters, through you, in my life, home, parenting, and in my children—even though they never had the opportunity to know you. Your letters of love (via God's love) show up everywhere.

The Cardinals are losing, Mom. Maybe they took the pitcher out too soon. I want you to know that I'm winning, even though I selfishly think you were taken out too early. Sometimes it's hard to realize you're gone because your heaven-sent letters are written on my heart. God's letters through you taught me and so many others what love, hope, and true happiness are all about. Your Spirit-written letters speak for themselves.

Father to Father: Thank You, Father, for Spirited mothers who write letters and who teach their children to read. Amen.

God's Man in Action: Tell your mom how much you appreciate and love her. If she is waiting for you in heaven, write her anyway.

My Father's Eyes

2 Corinthians 5:16

Recently a woman told my sons that it was obvious to her, because of their similar looks, that they were brothers. Then she looked at me, and it was obvious that I was their father. Some families pass on very strong genes from generation to generation. My mother's side of the family is that way. Today it can be difficult to match up family traits as so many people turn to plastic surgery, dyed hair, and other body-altering methods. But naturally, we don't have control over the fact that we may have our mother's nose or our father's eyes.

Contemporary Christian artist Amy Grant made the song "My Father's Eyes" popular. In the song she sings of having her father's eyes. Eye color is a genetic trait, but the lyrics don't refer to genetics. They focus on having the eyes of our heavenly Father.

What a blessing to have the eyes of our heavenly Father and His Son, Jesus Christ. When we have our heavenly Father's eyes, we also have His heart. The view from God's heavenly eyes is completely different than our worldly view. What a gift to look at others in the way our Father looks at them! What a joy to have the same view of ourselves as God has of us! His look is graceful. His view is heavenly. His focus is never blurred. Oh, to have our Father's eyes! What a trait to desire and have.

Our Father looks at everyone as His prize creation. His look is one of unconditional love seen perfectly in His Son's redemptive work on Calvary's cross. He looks in compassion. His eyes see hope in what we envision as a hopeless situation. His eyes and heart are filled with love when our natural response would be hatred. He rejoices with His creation, for He created the reasons for rejoicing. He sees potential when we potentially see nothing. He sees forgiven sinners when we only see the sin of sinners. Yes, He sees our handicaps inside and out, but He also knows that with His help we are capable of accomplishing the impossible.

Oh, to have our Father's eyes! For that prayer to become reality, we need to first see Jesus. We need to see how He lived and died, how He dealt with others, how He loved, and how He saw something when others saw nothing. We need to catch His vision.

That comes by walking daily with Him. It means sitting at His feet while He teaches us through His Word. It means talking with Him and watching for His response. It means allowing Him to lift our heads so He can look us in the eyes and place His body and blood within our lives through His Holy Meal.

God has a vision for helping, encouraging, and strengthening the faith of everyone around Him. Desire that vision. Let us not regard anyone from a worldly point of view. God focuses in on all our needs, but our faith is of first importance to Him. May our eyes see beyond outward appearances and into the fragile, saving faith of each person. Oh, to have our Father's eyes!

What a wonderful compliment if someone says to you, "I see you have your Father's eyes!" Celebrate that gift which has been passed on to you from heaven.

Father to Father: I want to see Jesus. For in His eyes I see His Father's eyes. I desire to look at others, myself, and all Your creation with Your eyes, Father. Jesus is carrying this request to You, for it is in His name that I pray and have vision. Amen.

God's Man in Action: The next time you see someone who is living his faith and acting with compassion and love, tell him, "It's obvious whose family you belong to. You have your Father's eyes."

On a Fishin' Mission

Luke 5:1–11

It was a fishin' mission that my children and I were on one afternoon. Just down the road from our house was a pond filled with algae and, we hoped, some fish. Now I'm not much of a fisherman, but I did my best to act as though I knew what I was doing. We packed a can of corn for bait. (Yes, I remembered to open the can before we left.) The cartoon character bobbers were attached to the line. The hooks were in order (and not in someone's hair), so we headed down the road for our fishin' mission. With our poles slung over our shoulders, we probably looked like a cross between Andy, Opie, and the Three Stooges.

At the pond we found out they were really biting—both the mosquitoes and the fish. Right and left we pulled them out of the water. It didn't take much effort because the largest was only about five inches long. (Hors d'oeuvres, maybe?) The fish must have been starving. It was exciting, fun, and smelly. Mission accomplished!

You have to have a mission when you go fishin'. The mission should be to catch fish. If not, can it be a true fishin' mission?

Jesus had a mission when He sent the disciples out fishin'. As Luke records the story, Jesus first helped them to accomplish their mission by providing such a large catch of fish that their nets began to break. He didn't stop there. He gave them another fishin' mission. "From now on," He said, "you will catch men."

Notice that He didn't say they would "try" to catch people. He provided them with the certainty of catching others within the net of His saving Gospel. Their focus on this new fishin' mission was strong. Scripture tells us that they left everything and followed Him. No questions. No details. No fear. They responded immediately. This fishin' mission would become their way of life. Even though many of them had spent their lives fishing, they had a lot to learn about this new catch they would be hauling in. They would learn from the Master Fisherman. They would practice fishing for others.

And they would catch "fish." No doubt about it. For they had the bait the world was craving—the Gospel of Jesus Christ. They had eternal news of hope and peace, joy, companionship, forgiveness, and renewed vision.

We have the same call to go with Jesus on a fishin' mission. We need the type of commitment the disciples had as we take our lead from the Master Fisherman. God's fishin' mission is a way of life. And the results will be the same because God is faithful to His Word.

I think we'll be amazed one day when the Lord tells

us of the wonderful casting job we did as a Christian family when we prayed together before supper in the restaurant; when our love for one another was obvious in a mall filled with broken families, hearts, and dreams; when we took time to share our blessings with other families. Let us also be amazed at His forgiving grace when we fail to fulfill His mission.

Fishing is a daily adventure with the Lord. "Don't be afraid," Jesus said to Peter and to us. Enjoy the fishin' mission. Plan to fish. Live daily with the fishin' mission in your heart and mind. There's a sea of starving people out there. Jesus has given our families the means to feed them. We're on a daily family fishin' mission. It won't be completed until we get to heaven and hear our Savior's voice say, "Mission accomplished! Well done, my good and faithful fishers of men."

Father to Father: Father, daily use my family as we live Your fishin' mission. With the Holy Spirit's guidance, may we be a bold witness of Your eternal gifts as You catch others through us. Amen.

God's Man in Action: Place a fishing lure, bobber, or a printed copy of the Matthew 28:18–20 fishin' mission in your home, car, or workplace to remind You of God's mission for your life.

Who Has the Answer?

1 Peter 3:15

Benjamin walked up to me and said, "Dad, I need some help with my science homework." Without missing a beat, he looked up at me and added, "Never mind, I'll ask Mom." My ego was deflated, flying around the room like an escaped balloon. Then I remembered telling him once that science wasn't my best subject, so he might want to ask Mom for more articulate answers to questions in that particular field.

Parents need to be ready to answer children with inquisitive, growing minds. Depending on your situation, home may not be the only place where others look to you for answers. Providing correct, precise, and articulate answers can add pressure to life. It's okay, by the way, to admit that you don't know the answer.

But there is one answer that God wants us to know and to be able to articulate to others. The apostle Peter writes, "Always be prepared to give an answer to everyone who asks you to give the reason for the hope that you have" (1 Peter 3:15).

All around us people desperately search for some hope in what seems to be hopeless situations. In Jesus Christ we have the answer. He is our hope. He provides us with a sure and certain hope through His life and love. With the living Christ, there is no such thing as a hopeless situation (although Satan would love for us to think otherwise). People are looking for hope in all the wrong places. That is why God tells us to always be prepared to give the reason for the hope we have.

My mother was prepared to tell the reason for her hope. One winter, a newspaper reporter was standing in front of her. She was five months pregnant with me. She had three stepchildren whose mother had died of cancer. In one week my mom and dad were to celebrate their first wedding anniversary. It was four days before Christmas. Her husband, my father, had just died from burns sustained in an accident at work. For many, the situation would seem hopeless.

The reporter asked her how she would be able to go on. Prepared to give the reason for the hope that she had, she responded, "I don't know exactly, but I do know that with God's help, we will make it." The reporter obviously missed the facts. His article stated that when he asked my mom how she would go on, he quoted her as saying, "I don't know—somehow." He left God out of his article and her answer.

What is important to me is that she was prepared to share her hope. She was able to articulate it in the midst of a difficult time. More than that, she taught her children to be prepared to answer anyone who asks about the reason for our hope. Today I have the privilege of preparing my children to give the answer of hope to a hopeless world.

It's important that my children know answers to the questions that arise as they study God's world through subjects such as math, science, history, English, and social studies. But it's more important to me and to my Father that they know the answer to the hope that we have.

That hope is found in Jesus Christ, who gave us His life, forgiveness, and resurrection victory. With Him, hopelessness has vanished. Hope now rises out of the ashes around us. What a message to carry with us into every situation, living it and sharing it.

Father to Father: Prepare me, Father, to always be able to share the reason for the hope I have through Jesus Christ, in whose name I place my hope and pray. Amen.

God's Man in Action: Write your answer to the question "What is the reason for the hope you have while living in a sinful, hurting world?" Write it to prepare yourself to speak it to someone in need of God's daily and eternal hope.

Future Changes

Malachi 4:6

The future just isn't what it used to be." Those words were credited to one of the most quoted people to ever live—Anonymous. For Christian fathers (and those who love them) the words take on special meaning. Because of our heavenly Father's love, shown perfectly in Jesus Christ, our future just isn't what it used to be.

That statement sounds like something Peter might have said. I can almost hear him say that after he found out that His crucified Savior, Jesus, was alive. Picture Peter and the other disciples locked in a room on Easter morning, doing nothing but coloring their future bleak. Out of the blue comes a banging on the door and news that raised new questions. Running to the tomb, Peter must have wondered if his friend's body was stolen or if Jesus had stolen Satan's thunder and risen from the dead. When he finally realized that Jesus was alive, I can imagine him shouting to the world, "The future just isn't what it used to be!"

Peter had felt like this before. This man, whose goals once may have included the Fisherman Hall of Fame, found his future drastically changed because a man named Jesus said to him, "Follow Me." When the Son of God healed Peter's mother-in-law, the future wasn't what it used to be for his family. Peter's confession that Jesus was the Christ, the Son of the living God, caused his future to be something it wasn't before. There was the look Jesus shared with him in the courtyard when Peter disowned Jesus. The look told Peter that although his sin was exposed, Jesus owned a treasure entitled "Forgiveness and Grace." Peter was also a witness to the death and resurrection of Jesus Christ. Indeed, his future wasn't what it used to be.

Jesus Christ changes lives. He heals past hurts. He gives courage for present realities. He causes our future to be something it didn't used to be. This truth continues to echo out of the empty tomb and into our lives. We must place our lives, trust, and hope in Him.

The future just isn't what it used to be. What a blessing it would be if those words were printed on wallpaper in every birthing room where men and women become mothers and fathers.

Every father who lifts up prayers for his children knows that the future isn't what it used to be because God's answers will guide them daily.

Fathers and families who have failed in their callings are led to repentance to receive the peace of God through full forgiveness. Their futures are not what they used to be.

The future of fathers who have stood over a loved

one's casket isn't what it used to be because their risen Savior says, "Because I live, you and your loved one shall live."

I pray that every fellow father who thinks he is facing a dead end would take these words of hope to heart while placing his hope in Christ. My prayer is the same for those held hostage in foreign lands or in the jungles of the business world; those in prisons of sin and prisons with bars; those riding through life in a rut and those taking a detour that seems to have no end; those in debt and those who owe someone an apology—people everywhere who are coloring their future bleak.

Rejoice with Christians in the hope found in our living and life-giving Lord. Our future, our family's future, and that of future Christian fathers is bright and glorious because of Jesus Christ and the love of our heavenly Father. With Christ as our living Lord, the prophecy of future days is being fulfilled: "He will turn the hearts of the fathers to their children, and the hearts of the children to their fathers" (Malachi 4:6). The future just isn't what it used to be!

Father to Father: Father, I am eternally grateful that my future isn't what it used to be because of Your perfect love in Jesus Christ. Turn my heart towards You and Your children. Amen.

God's Man in Action: Immediately pray for someone who is painting their future bleak. Lift them to the Father's care and pray that God would use you to be His messenger of hope.

Bedside Thoughts

Psalm 121:2

It's nearing midnight. My children have been asleep for several hours now. After spending some quiet time sitting on their beds, these are some of my random bedside thoughts.

- A few hours ago I prayed that the Lord and His angels would surround the three of you tonight. I wonder how many angels the Lord brought with Him. Is this holy ground as I sit in this angel's room?

- I wish I could put my ear to your head and listen to your dreams.

- You are growing so very fast. I remember when we put you in your first big bed with the railing. This big bed doesn't look so big anymore, but you do.

- I should have apologized for losing my patience with you today. You were just excited about doing something with me. You had spent the day in school and finally had a chance to run and shout. You have so much energy. I regret that I missed that time together. I will ask for your forgiveness tomorrow. I will ask

God's forgiveness right now.

- Speaking of such energy, it's amazing to see your bodies so still after a day of running, talking, skipping rope, playing games, eating. Now your bodies rest. You need it. God didn't create you with bionic bodies. I have much to learn from you. The day is for work (and play in your case) and the night is for sleeping.

- When I tucked you in, I said, "Sleep tight." I should have told you, "Sleep loose." You'll have enough stress later in life that will cause sleep-tight nights. Sleep at peace.

- I really enjoyed our bedtime songfest. I'm certain the angels we invited joined along as our backup singers. I wonder if they can sing and smile at the same time?

- Your room is filled with memories: books and more books that have closed out many of your days; trophies; pictures; souvenirs … memories of days past. As you grow older, I wonder what you will remember and what things you won't recall that your mom and I hoped you would.

- These growing, resting bodies of yours are such miracles. It's amazing the things your brains are taking in for the very first time. You marvel at so much. To adults everything's old hat. We miss the marvel. Keep reminding me to marvel.

- Benjamin, I love the gift of your imagination in which you saw an entire secret fort in the mountains. You created it out of blankets and boxes for your brother and sister, but your mom and I enjoyed it just as much.

- Sarah, thank you for the wonderful chalk pictures on the driveway that welcomed me home today. They were bright, creative, fun. Tonight's rain will wash them away, but I'll keep a copy in my mental box of memories.

- Christopher, that giggle spree you went on during supper when I did something silly made my week. Thank you.

- I love you—each of you—very, very much.

- Dear Guardian Lord, there is no need to close my eyes when I pray tonight for I'm looking into Your eyes through these children. Thank You for sending the angels—the ones I can't see and the ones named Benjamin, Sarah, and Christopher. Keep these children marveling at Your creation as they continue to teach me to marvel as well. Help me love them as You love them. Amen.

Father to Father: Father, as I reflect on the gift of my family, I see that they are reflections of Your grace. For that I am very grateful. Amen.

God's Man in Action: Take time tonight to sit next to your sleeping children. Reflect and rejoice!